Hold'em Poker

For Advanced Players

By
David Sklansky AND Mason Malmuth

A product of Two Plus Two Publishing

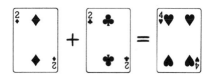

SECOND EDITION
FIRST PRINTING: 1994

Printing and Binding
Creel Printing Co.
Las Vegas, Nevada

Printed in the United States of America

HOLD'EM POKER FOR ADVANCED PLAYERS

For information contact:

Two Plus Two Publishing
Las Vegas, NV
(702) 796-9487

ISBN: 1-880685-01-9

Table of Contents

Foreword by Ray Zee vi

Introduction 1

Using This Book 5

Why Play Texas Hold'em? 7

Part One: The First Two Cards 9
    Introduction 10
    Hand Rankings 12
    The First Two Cards: Early Position 16
    The First Two Cards: Middle Position 21
    The First Two Cards: Late Position 23
    The First Two Cards: Live Blinds 28
    The First Two Cards: Late-Position Blind 34
    Afterthought 36

Part Two: Strategic Concepts 39
    Introduction 40
    Semi-Bluffing 41
    The Free Card 49
    Slow-Playing 59
    Check-Raising 62
    Odds and Implied Odds 66
    Bluffing 69
    Inducing Bluffs 72
    Folding When the Pot is Big 75
    Heads-up Versus Multiway 77
    Raising 79
    Heads-up on Fifth Street 85
    Afterthought 92

Part Three:Miscellaneous Topics 93
   Introduction 94
   Being Beat on the River 95
   Continuing the Semi-Bluff 98
   Getting a Free Card 100
   Staying With a Draw 101
   Playing When There Is No Raise Before the Flop . . 103
   Playing When Two Suited Cards Flop 105
   Playing When a Pair Flops 106
   Playing Pairs in the Hole 107
   Playing Trash Hands 110
   Playing Against a Maniac 112
   Playing Good Hands When It Is Three Bets Before the
     Flop 114
   Playing When the Flop Is All the Same Suit 116
   Fourth Street Play 118
   Afterthought 123

Part Four: Playing in Non-Standard Games 124
   Introduction 125
   Playing in Loose Games 126
   Playing in Extremely Tight Games 128
   Playing Against a Live Straddle 129
   Playing in Short-Handed Games 131
   Playing in Spread-Limit Games 133
   Afterthought 135

Part Five: Other Skills 136
   Introduction 137
   Reading Hands 138
   Psychology 144
   Afterthought 150

Part Six: Questions and Answers 151
   Introduction 152
   Afterthought 201

Conclusion 203

Appendix A: Probability 205

Appendix B: Glossary 209

Foreword

by Ray Zee

Texas Hold'em is hard. There is probably no other form of poker as difficult. Yet, the game appears deceptively simple. Many players, even after much experience at the poker tables, still play as though any two cards can win. Of course, those who play in this fashion quickly lose their money.

The book you are holding, written by David Sklansky and Mason Malmuth, will have far-reaching effects on the poker world. Simply put, no matter where Texas hold'em is played, it will now be a much tougher game to beat.

If you are a serious player, this means that unless you study the strategies and techniques in this text, you will be left behind. If you are new to the game but are willing to put in the requisite time and effort, you soon will be more proficient at this form of poker than many of today's professional players. However, don't expect to become an expert overnight.

In *Hold'em Poker For Advanced Players,* the authors provide not only numerous sophisticated concepts, but lots of examples as well. Many of these advanced ideas have never before appeared correctly in print. In fact, numerous concepts contained in this book are well-understood only by a very small group of players — extremely successful players, I might add.

This brings up another point. This is one of the very few poker books actually written by winning players, and the authors thoroughly explain the techniques that have made them so successful at the tables. In addition, I know both authors quite well, and I know that no winning information was held back.

Actually, I have mixed feelings about seeing this book published. I'm not in favor of anything that will make the poker games tougher to beat. On the other hand, *Hold'em Poker for Advanced Players* should help to spread this extremely interesting game and to make it even more popular.

Consequently, I guess it is for the best that this book is now available.

Finally, let me repeat that the techniques and ideas offered in this text should make any disciplined and studious player a significant winner. However, as already stated, it won't happen overnight. Most players will have to reread the book and study the concepts many times. In fact, I suspect that some of you will literally wear the covers off your copies of *Hold'em Poker for Advanced Players*. But I know that those of you who do will be very happy with your results.

Special note: The authors would like to thank Ray Zee for sharing many of his concepts and ideas with us. Because of Ray, this text is a better work.

Introduction

Texas hold'em is perhaps the most complicated of poker games. This is because it is rare to be absolutely clear about the exact manner in whicl hand should be played. It is not uncommon to hear two expert players debate the pros and cons of a certain strategy. This means that even though you are about to read solid guidelines to winning, the strategies given are not set in concrete and under certain conditions, the best strategies may be different from those that are recommended.

On the other hand, the strategies in this text definitely provide a strong winning approach. If this were not the case, neither author would be in a position to write this book, simply because we would both be broke and standing on the rail.

The "winning approach" we provide is a tight but aggressive one. It is not a "fast" approach, which some experts use to win slightly more money. The reason for this is simply that most players who attempt to play fast will fail, as they do not have the judgment to handle the many situations that come up where they have put themselves in jeopardy. In any case, becoming an expert hold'em player, even with the help of this book, will not be easy. It will require not only a great deal of study, but also a great deal of thinking, plus many hours of playing time at the hold'em tables.

Keep in mind that the following strategies are designed for medium limit games, that is $10-$20 hold'em up to (and including) $30-$60 hold'em. In smaller games, many of the sophisticated plays, used to manipulate opponents into making errors do not work, simply because most of your opponents are not aware enough to be tricked. Also, the structure of smaller games is proportionately different. In spite of this, many ideas in the book will help you in smaller games while you work your way up to the bigger ones. As for the bigger hold'em games, where players are capable of thinking at many different levels, an understanding of the information in this book, combined

1

with a great deal of experience and some hard thinking about the game, is the only way to guarantee success.

Before the first edition of *Hold'em Poker for Advanced Players* was published, we debated for a long time before deciding to release this information. We thought the strategies presented would make many of the games we played in much tougher, and we both derive much of our income from playing poker. However, after considering the avalanche of hold'em books — most of which were inaccurate — that was reaching the market, we believed it was only right to go ahead and produce the text.

Incidentally, the first edition of *Hold'em Poker for Advanced Players* was not meant to replace *Hold'em Poker* by David Sklansky. In fact, we still consider that book absolutely must reading for anyone interested in learning the game. However, we intended to update many of the ideas in the original Sklansky work to reflect today's modern structure and players, as well as to delve into much more sophisticated strategy.

You are now reading the second edition of *Hold'em Poker for Advanced Players*. It has been six years since the first edition appeared, and much has happened during that time. First of all, poker — and hold'em in particular — has exploded across the country. This means that if you become proficient at Texas hold'em, there are many good games to play in and lots of places where these games can be found.

But the games have changed from the time this text first appeared. Specifically, players who just play tight don't seem to be as prevalent as they used to be. Moreover, there are now many more players who play very aggressively (perhaps overly so), and loose, action play has become much more common. In fact, hold'em pots frequently become quite large, with a great deal of money sometimes going into the center of the table before the flop.

There are probably many reasons why this has happened, but it is clear to us that this text had a lot to do with it. Many of the plays that we explain — and that we only rarely saw before — are now commonplace. On the other hand, with numerous new players at the hold'em tables, many of whom come to "gamble," it is no wonder that the pace of the games has accelerated.

This change doesn't really affect the strategies that *Hold'em Poker for Advanced Players* provides, but it does affect when certain concepts come into play. As we pointed out six years ago, there is no substitute for experience, and to ensure success, you should be doing a great deal of thinking about the game.

The main difference between this edition and the first edition of the book is that we give more examples and offer more detailed explanations. But the basic concepts from the first edition remain the same.

Finally, we would like to express our appreciation to Lynne Loomis for editing this work. Thanks to her, our ideas are now more clearly stated and thus should be more easily understood.

Using This Book

As stated in the introduction, this book will require you to do a great deal of thinking. It is recommended that the whole book be read first, then you can return to those sections that require more study. Also, you should memorize the hand rankings and how to play the first two cards. We see no better way to master this area of hold'em play. However, after you have gained the requisite experience, you will begin to see where it is appropriate to deviate from "correct" strategy. Almost all top players do this, although you should not get carried away. The text will supply some hints in this area.

We also recommend that you not jump right into a $30-$60 game. Even though the strategies in this book will win their share at the $30-$60 limit, especially if your opposition is not too tough, it is still better to start lower and work your way up. In a game as complex as Texas hold'em, there is no substitute for experience.

Keep in mind when trying to master hold'em that at times many of the following concepts will seem to contradict each other. For example, some concepts might recommend that you bet your hand right out, while other concepts will advise you to go for a check-raise. One of the keys to successful hold'em play is to learn how to balance these ideas, which will help you to select the best strategy the vast majority of the time.

Finally, the game that we address (unless otherwise noted) is a structured-limit game. This game has two blinds, both to the dealer's left, with the first (small) blind being either one-half or two-thirds the size of the second (big) blind. All bets and raises before the flop and on the flop are equal to the size of the big blind, and all bets and raises on fourth street (known as the turn) and fifth street (known as the river) are double the size of the big blind. If you play in a game with a different structure, some of the ideas and concepts that this text discusses will not be totally accurate. However, the section titled "Non-standard Games" should help you in this area.

Why Play Texas Hold'em?

There are many forms of poker, and you can win money at virtually all of them if you develop the right set of skills. So why learn to play Texas hold'em? Why is this the game of the future? And why, of all poker games, is this complex form your best bet?

The answer is easy. By playing hold'em, the expert player can win the most money with a reasonable amount of risk.

You win money at poker because of two important factors. First, some of your opponents play badly, and in extreme cases, literally give their money away. This seems to happen frequently in Texas hold'em, since any two cards can win. However, random hands do not win often enough to show a profit, and when they do win, they frequently must be played cautiously which also minimizes their profitability. In addition, hands that appear similar in strength to the non-skilled player are often quite different from each other. For example, holding just an ace does not make your hand very strong. Yet players who do not understand these basic ideas seem to flock to hold'em games. (If you want to verify this statement, just look at the hold'em explosion that took place in California when the game became legal in 1987.)

The second reason you can win money when playing hold'em is that this form of poker offers numerous opportunities for the expert player to make expert plays that extract additional money from unsuspecting opponents. This is less true of most other forms of poker.

We earlier mentioned that the risk factor in hold'em is reasonable. The correct way to assess risk in a poker game is through a statistical measure known as the standard deviation. We won't discuss the standard deviation in detail here (see *Gambling Theory and Other Topics* by Mason Malmuth) but will reiterate that it is a measure of the amount of short-term luck in a game.

Specifically, the poorer the relationship between the expectation (win rate) and the standard deviation the larger the fluctuations that you — the skilled player — can go through. Or, put another way, the worse you can run. Consequently, you usually should prefer a poker game where your bankroll requirements when compared to the size of the game, are not too steep.

There is no question that once you have achieved expert status, hold'em offers an excellent relationship between the expectation and the standard deviation. The reasons for this are that the best hand holds up more often in hold'em than in any other game and that you have the advantage of being able to see your opponent's last card. This means that sometimes you can throw away a hand that you would have to call with in other forms of poker, or you might be able to get in an extra bet, whereas in other games you might be forced to check.[1]

Of course, hold'em can still be very frustrating — especially when it seems as though your opponents are always making their two- or three-out hands. However, with the tremendous growth of hold'em, along with what we have just stated, there is no question that anyone who becomes an expert at this game will do very well indeed.

---

[1]This relationship is not as good as it used to be in some middle-limit games, where a great deal of money goes into the pot before the flop.

Part One

The First Two Cards

The First Two Cards

Introduction

The one area of hold'em play where many strict guidelines can be given is on the first two cards. This is because the number of possible combinations is not that great. However, this does not mean that every hand should be played the same way every time, or that playing the first two cards is easy. You occasionally should play a hand differently not only for the sake of variation, but also because of the type of game you are in. Expert players must be fooled more often than poor ones. But even if poor players always have a good idea of exactly where you are, you will lose some of your edge.

Also, how loose and passive the game is can make a significant difference. Some hands that are not usually profitable to play become significant money winners if your opponents are non-aggressive. The opposite is also true. Hands that are normally worth a play should be discarded if a couple of very aggressive players are in the game, particularly if these players know what they are doing.

In addition, how well you play is very important. As your judgment improves, you should be able to play a few more hands than these guidelines suggest. But don't go overboard with this concept. Always remember tight, aggressive play will get the money. This is true no matter what you may observe in the short run. Sometimes you will see bad players taking down pot after pot. In the short run, their play can look terrific. But in the long run, this type of play does not get the money.

And finally, before we get started, keep in mind that hold'em is a game that easily can cause you to go "on tilt." For instance, a hand like can be very tempting to play even from an early position, especially if you are losing.

A unique aspect of hold'em is that hands you *don't* play can sometimes be frustrating, because the board is always the same whether you play or not. There will be occasions when you would have made a strong hand had you not thrown away your cards. Do not let this affect you. Even though any two cards can win, random holdings don't win often enough to be profitable.

Hand Rankings

To simplify the presentation of some of the strategies that follow, the starting hands have been placed in appropriate groupings. The reason for this is that most of the hands in each grouping can be played roughly the same before the flop. However, there are many exceptions, which will be discussed in the text.

These hand rankings (with some modifications) first appeared in David Sklansky's book *Essays on Poker*. (*Essays on Poker* is today published as part of *Sklansky on Poker*.) They are slightly different from the rankings that appear in Sklansky's original book *Hold'em Poker*. The alterations reflect the structure change from one small blind to two blinds which causes more multiway pots and higher pot odds — especially on the flop. Also reflected is the fact that the players have become tougher and generally more aggressive as the years have gone by.

This has raised the value of suited hands, especially suited connectors. Medium pairs also have gone up in value, because you no longer should automatically give up when an overcard flops, especially if the pot is being contested short-handed.

The rankings are as follows, with an "s" indicating suited and an "x" indicating a small card. Note that a 10 is represented as "T." Also, if no "s" appears, then the hand is not suited. (These notations will be used throughout this book.)

Group 1: AA, KK, QQ, JJ, AKs

Group 2: TT, AQs, AJs, KQs, AK

Group 3: 99, JTs, QJs, KJs, ATs, AQ

Group 4: T9s, KQ, 88, QTs, 98s, J9s, AJ, KTs

Group 5: 77, 87s, Q9s, T8s, KJ, QJ, JT, 76s, 97s, Axs, 65s

Group 6: 66, AT, 55, 86s, KT, QT, 54s, K9s, J8s, 75s

Group 7: 44, J9, 43s, T9, 33, 98, 64s, 22, Kxs, T7s, Q8s

Group 8: 87, 53s, A9, Q9, 76, 42s, 32s, 96s, 85s, J8, J7s, 65, 54, 74s, K9, T8

These rankings reflect not only which group each starting hand belongs to but its approximate order in that group as well. In reality, it's usually necessary to know only which group a starting hand is in. Consequently, Tables I and II provide an easier scheme for memorizing the group for each starting hand. Any hand not listed in the tables is ranked below Group 8.

Table I: Hand Groupings for Pairs

Hand	Group	Hand	Group
AA	1	77	5
KK	1	66	6
QQ	1	55	6
JJ	1	44	7
TT	2	33	7
99	3	22	7
88	4		

Table II: Hand Groupings For Non-Pairs

Hand	Group		Hand	Group	
	Suited	Not Suited		Suited	Not Suited
AK	1	2	98	4	7
AQ	2	3	97	5	-
AJ	2	4	96	8	-
AT	3	6			
A9	5	8	87	5	8
Ax	5	-	86	6	-
			85	8	-
KQ	2	4			
KJ	3	5	76	5	8
KT	4	6	75	6	-
K9	6	8	74	8	-
Kx	7	-			
			65	5	8
QJ	3	5	64	7	-
QT	4	6			
Q9	5	8	54	6	8
Q8	7	-	53	8	-
JT	3	5	43	7	-
J9	4	7	42	8	-
J8	6	8			
J7	8	-	32	8	-
T9	4	7			
T8	5	8			
T7	7	-			

It is very important to memorize these groupings, especially if you are fairly new to hold'em poker. There is no way around this, and the tables make the task much easier. Once the tables are memorized, this system will facilitate applying many of the concepts that follow. (For those of you who are interested in the rationale behind these rankings, see *Hold'em Poker* by David Sklansky.)

The First Two Cards:
Early Position

Hold'em is a positional game, perhaps more so than any other form of poker. This is because the button determines the order in which players act for all betting rounds. (The only exception to this are the blinds, who act last on the first betting round but act first on all succeeding betting rounds.) Consequently, the number of hands that can be safely played from an early position — which we will define as the first three positions to the left of the big blind in a ten-handed game — is quite limited. Since you are out of position on all betting rounds, you need a superior starting hand to make it worth playing.[2]

Specifically, in early position in a typical hold'em game, if you are the first one in or if there is a call to your right, be prepared to play only those hands in the first four groups. In a loose game, as long as the players are not too aggressive, you can add the Group 5 hands, especially the suited connectors. In a tough game, it is probably best to discard even the Group 4 hands. These guidelines are very important. Playing too many hands up front is one of the most costly errors that you can make.

When we refer to a game as loose, we mean a game without much before-the-flop raising and with many players in most pots. When we say tough game, we mean one with a lot of raising but not many large multiway pots. There's also a type of game where several players play very well once the flop comes. If you are not sure what type of game you are playing in, it is best to assume that the game is typical until you can determine otherwise. Remember that big pots do not necessarily make a

---

[2]A fuller treatment of the importance of position can be found in both *Hold'em Poker* and *The Theory of Poker* by David Sklansky.

game good. If the big pots are created by a lot of raising, your best strategy might be to look for a softer game.

Sometimes you will need to add a few hands to those you play up front to throw your opponents off. For example, you occasionally should play a hand like

in an early position, even if the game is tough, to stop your more observant opponents from stealing against you when "rags" flop. However, make sure that your hand is suited, and do this only occasionally.

If there is a raise to your right and the game is typical or tough, you should limit your play to only those hands in Groups 1 and 2. Against an extremely tight player in a tough game, it may be correct to throw away some of the Group 2 hands, such as

and

(Remember that this chapter refers to early-position decisions.)

If there is a raise to your right and the game is loose, you should be able to safely play Group 3 hands as well. However, beware of AQ. Even in a loose game, this hand does not play well against an early-position raiser if many players remain to act behind you. (Of course, if the AQ is suited, you definitely would play the hand.)

If no one has yet called, almost always raise with AA, KK, QQ, AK, and AQ. Part of the reason to raise with these hands is that they lose much of their value in large multiway pots. If there have been callers, usually raise with hands in Groups 1 and 2, plus with some other hands at random. (Again, these random raises should be made only occasionally.)

Also, if no one has yet called, raise approximately two-thirds of the time with AKs, AQs, AJs, and KQs. The reason for sometimes calling with these hands is not only for deception purposes, but also because they play well in multiway pots. However, because of the large blind structure in today's game, which already encourages multiway play, it is not necessary to call with these hands very often. In fact, against weak opposition, it is best to raise with them, since the deception you are trying to gain by just calling won't do you much good anyway.

Finally, if no one has yet called, raise approximately one-third of the time with a hand like

This is mainly for deception purposes. Again, keep in mind how strong your competition is. If you are in a game full of extremely weak opponents, it is generally best to simply call with these hands.

By the way, if you call with a large suited connector and are raised, go ahead and reraise with AKs and possibly with AQs. In addition, if a lot of people are in the pot, you sometimes can reraise with a hand like

The reason for this last raise requires some explanation and will be better understood after you get further into the book. Basically, you are making the pot larger so that if you get a flop you like, such as two flush cards of the appropriate suit, then more of your opponents will be encouraged to stay for one or two more cards with as little as one overcard.

Let's return to loose games. Keep in mind that some hands, such as

or a small pair, play well against many opponents. If there are usually a lot of callers but not much raising, these types of hands become playable in early position. However, overplaying these hands up front — and most players do just that — can get you into trouble. Make sure that the requirement of a loose and passive game is met. Again, if you are not sure, it is usually best to pass on these hands in an early position.

One hand that we have not yet addressed is JJ. If no one has opened and you are in an early position, it is usually best to raise with JJ in a tight game and to just call with this hand in a loose game. With two jacks in the pocket, you would prefer either to have no more than one or two opponents in the hope that your hand holds up without improvement, or to have as many opponents as possible when the majority of your profits come from flopping three of a kind. The worst scenario is when *exactly* three or four opponents see the flop with you. This most likely will occur when you call in a tight game or raise in a loose game.

If you hold JJ and the pot has been raised and reraised before the action gets to you, you should fold. This is correct even when you are in a middle or late position. However, if you have opened with JJ and the pot has been raised and reraised behind you, then it is correct to go ahead and call. What you are hoping to do in this situation is to flop trips. If you do not make a set, be prepared to fold (although folding is not necessarily automatic).

The First Two Cards: Middle Position

How you play your hands from a middle position, which we will define as the fourth, fifth, and sixth positions to the left of the big blind, is similar to the play of your hands from an early position. The main difference is that you now can play a few more hands, since your positional disadvantage is not as great.

This means that in an unraised pot, you can play all hands in Groups 1-5 when the game is typical or tough. In a loose, passive game, it is all right to play the Group 6 hands as well. Also, if you are not the first one in, consider the strength of your opponents. Specifically, the weaker your opponents are, the more hands you can play. Put another way, you should be more inclined to play marginal hands against poorer players.

If the pot already has been raised, almost always reraise with AA, KK, QQ, AKs, and AK. In addition, occasionally reraise with other good hands, such as

or

Remember, these raises are made so you can vary your play and throw some of your opponents off. Raising too often with these types of hands could prove to be very expensive. Moreover, you usually should throw these hands away if the pot already has been raised.

One difference between early and middle position is that in middle position, you virtually never just call with the large suited connectors, such as

if you are the first one in. One of the reasons for this is that some of your opponents will begin to suspect you of trying to steal the blinds (with weak hands) when you raise after several people have passed. So you may as well raise all of those times when you hold a good hand.

Thus, if you are the first one in, raise with all hands that are in Groups 1, 2, and 3. This is also usually correct if there have been callers to your right. However, when there are callers, don't always raise with the Group 3 hands. If you hold a Group 3 hand, consider how well your opponents play and whether you want a lot of players or a few players. If your opponents are strong, tend to call; otherwise, raise. When you want a lot of opponents, such as with JTs as opposed to AQ, this is another time to just call (when you are not the first one in) with a Group 3 hand.

One strategy that begins to come into play in the middle positions is that you almost always should raise when no one has yet entered the pot, five or six players have passed, and you have a playable hand. If you think there is a reasonable chance, perhaps as small as 25 percent, that all players behind you (including the blinds) will fold, and you are the first one in, then you should raise with any hand in Groups 1-6.

The First Two Cards: Late Position

On the button and in the position just to the button's right (and sometimes in the position two to the button's right), much of what is correct play is quite different from what we have seen in the early and middle positions. One of the reasons for this is that you will have excellent position on all betting rounds which will enable you to make better decisions than you can make in the earlier positions. This is because when your opponents check or bet, you have gained a great deal of information about their hands, while they do not have this same information about your hand.

You should understand that if you are in late position and are the first player to enter the pot, any hand that you should play is almost always worth a raise. This usually means hands in Groups 1-7, maybe those in Group 8, and even worse hands if you think your opponents are tight enough that you have a decent chance to steal the blinds. If there are already callers, raise with hands in Groups 1-3 and sometimes with Group 4 hands. However, if there are many players, do not raise with unsuited high cards, but for reasons already mentioned, be somewhat inclined to raise with hands as weak as Group 5 if they are straight flush combinations.

For example, if you hold

and a lot of players are in the pot, it is probably best to just call (if there has not yet been a raise). On the other hand, if you have

several players are already in the pot, and no one has yet raised, then raising is certainly all right and often may be the best strategy to follow.

Another reason to raise is if you think it may "buy you the button." Being able to act last on succeeding betting rounds is a major advantage.

Sometimes you can raise with some weaker hands in late position. This opportunity arises when you are against one or two callers who did not enter the pot from the early positions (and thus probably have weak hands), and you have a playable hand that you would prefer to play against a small number of opponents. This would include hands like A7s, KJ, QJ, and even a hand as weak as QT.

One of the reasons for this type of raise is that against weak opposition (and, as usual, you always should consider your opponents when making your playing decisions), it allows you to take control of the pot. That is, if your opponents do not flop a hand, and you bet after they have checked, you often will be able to steal the pot. This is especially true if a high card has flopped. In addition, if you choose not to bet on the flop, your raise may have gained you a free card. (More on this later in the text.)

Here's an example of this idea. Suppose you raise a weak player who calls from a middle position, and you hold

If the flop comes something like

your opponent will likely check and fold, assuming that he does not flop anything, since he now will fear that you have a king.

To call a raise cold, you still need a very good hand, even in late position. However, if several people are already in the pot, even though it has been raised, you also can play hands like

and

In addition, almost always reraise with any Group 1 hand.

There is also a time when you would reraise with weaker hands, even those as weak as Group 4. This occurs when your opponent is the first one in from a late position and he enters the pot with a raise. Notice that your opponent may be trying to steal the blinds, and a reraise on your part with reasonably strong hands becomes correct. However, with the exception of AJ and KQ, reraise with a Group 4 hand only if your opponent is a weak player and you believe you have excellent control over him. Otherwise, you are probably better off to limit yourself to Groups 1-3 for this play. If neither you nor your opponent flops a hand, your raise not only may stop him from trying to steal the pot, but also may allow you to do the stealing. Keep in mind that in this situation, the correct play on your part is to either reraise or fold before the flop. It is almost never correct to just call.

If you are dead last — that is, if you are on the button — and there are already callers, you can play hands in Groups 1 - 7. If you have a small pair and are against four or five callers, the correct play is to sometimes raise. This is another example of making the pot larger so that if you hit your hand, your opponents may be more inclined to call you with just overcards on the flop. In addition, they all may check to you, thus giving you a free card and another (small) chance to make your set. Also, this play is sometimes correct with small suited connectors. Again, don't get carried away with these plays. But making them occasionally can be very effective.

If you are on the button, a lot of players are already in, and the pot is not raised, you can call with many additional hands. This includes those hands in Group 8 and even hands as weak as

The reason for this is the tremendous implied odds that you will be getting if the flop comes just as you would like for it to

come. However, don't take this idea too far. It is unlikely that it ever would be correct to call with a hand like

As already mentioned, if no one has called, you can raise the blinds from the last position (button) with any hand in Groups 1-8. With a hand like an ace with an unsuited weak kicker, you still should raise the blinds if they are either very tight or very weak players. When we say weak, we are referring to a player who will let your ace win in a showdown. For example, suppose you raise with something like

and are called by the blind. If this person is willing to check on the river with nothing, even if you show weakness by not betting on the turn, then he is the type of player you would be happy to play a lone ace against.

The same is true with a hand like Kx, but even more so. That is, against typical opposition, usually pass with Kx. However, if you do play a hand like Kx on the button, make sure that you always raise. Never just call the blind if you are the first one in.

The First Two Cards: Live Blinds

Playing your first two cards out of the blinds is very different from the other positions, because you will have terrible position for the next three rounds, but this is somewhat compensated for by the fact that you have to call only a partial bet. This makes you play extremely tight in some situations but enables you to play extremely loose in others.

Over their careers, many players lose a lot of money from the blind positions. This is because they frequently overestimate the value of their hand in comparison to the partial bet that they are required to make to continue playing. Even though you can play looser in some situations, you still must play fairly tight if the pot has been raised and the raiser is not in a steal position.

Assume you are in the (live) big blind and no one else has raised. In this situation, you usually should raise only with extremely good hands. Remember, one of the reasons to raise in late positions, is to help you to take control of the pot. However, this is much harder to do when you are first to act on the flop.

Let's suppose you have

and one or two aggressive players have called from an early position. Your best play usually (but not always) is to call and (perhaps) to try for a check-raise later. You don't have to hit your hand to make check-raising the correct play. You just need to be fairly sure that the flop did not help anyone. An example might be a flop like

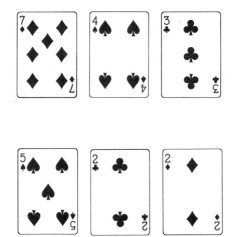

or

Since these were early-position players, there is an excellent chance that you have the best hand. You can check-raise if you think someone with a hand that is worse than your AK will bet in this spot.

However, if you hold AK in the big blind and are called by only one or two players from *late* positions, then you usually should raise. Because of their positions — and implied weakness when they just call — you cannot rule out any flop from hitting them. However, a raise is now the best play, since it is likely that your hand is far superior.

It also is correct to raise in the big blind when several people have called and you hold a hand like JTs, T9s, or a small pair. Now, for the same reasons as previously discussed, a raise may become correct. Keep in mind that this play is not as strong from the blind position, because you will be unlikely to get a free card if you check. However, if the flop does come as you would like, your raise may entice some players to stay with hands that they should fold if they knew what you held. (See *The Theory of Poker* by David Sklansky for more discussion of this idea.)

Suppose you are the big blind, the pot has been called on your left, and someone now raises on your right. In this case, you should call only with your better hands. This is because you can be reraised on your left. But if many players are in the pot, you should play more hands, especially hands that have the potential to make big hands, such as straight and flush draws. This would include hands like

and

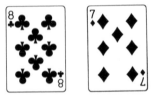

Also, if the raise is on your left, you can once again call with a few more hands, since you do not fear a reraise.

When the pot is raised and you are in the big blind, one hand that demands special attention is KJ. The reason for this is that a hand such as

can easily make a second-best hand that you will have to pay off all the way. This does not mean that you can never call a legitimate raise with KJ, but it does mean that the typical player calls much too often with this hand. Again, this is one of those situations where knowing your opponent can be a crucial factor in determining the correct decision. (AT is another hand in this category with similar problems.)

If the pot has been raised but there are a lot of players, you can begin to play hands like

and

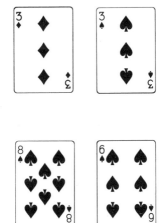

out of either blind position. And, of course, you usually would reraise with AA or KK when you are in either blind. But as already discussed, don't automatically reraise with AK (or QQ, for that matter).

One situation where big-blind play changes drastically occurs when you are against a possible steal-raise — that is, a raise from a late position by a player who you think would attempt to pick up the blinds with a weak hand. Remember, against a legitimate raise, you still need a fairly good hand to call. In fact, a good guideline is to call with essentially the same hands that you normally would cold call with if you were in a late position. But a steal-raise is a different matter.

Against weak opponents, who won't make good use of their positional advantage on the flop, you can call in the big blind with hands as weak as those in Group 8. However, if someone calls in between you and your opponent, or if your opponent plays well, then you must tighten up some. But you still can play a lot of hands, perhaps Groups 1-6.

Many of these same comments also apply to the little blind. However, when you call a raise from the little blind, not only do you have to put a larger fraction of a bet into the pot, but also a player remains to act behind you. One situation where correct little-blind play differs from big-blind play is against a possible steal-raise. Now if you are going to play (usually with a hand in Groups 1-6), you just about always should reraise. The purpose of this reraise is to drive the big blind out of the pot. However, if there is also a caller or a cold caller, then this play is usually incorrect without an excellent hand, because you now know that at least one of your opponents is likely to have a legitimate hand. In addition, you should, as usual, consider how well your opponent plays. Remember, the better he plays, the higher quality hand you need to make this type of play.

There are two other spots where little-blind play differs from big-blind play. The first occurs when the pot is not raised and it will cost you only a fraction of a bet to play. If the fraction to enter the pot is half a bet, then you (the player in the little blind) should still be somewhat selective of the hands you play, though you should play loose. For example, hands like

any two suited cards, or a hand that contains an ace are probably all right to call with. But hands like still should be thrown away. However, if it costs only one-third of a bet to enter the pot, every hand should be played. In this spot, it is just too cheap to throw away your hand, no matter how bad it is. The one exception occurs when the big blind is a frequent raiser. Why waste even one-third of a bet, since you have to fold if he raises.

The other situation that is unique to the little blind is when everyone has thrown away his hand. The question now is whether to fold, call the big blind, or raise the big blind. In addition to the ideas in the previous paragraph, keep in mind that for all four betting rounds, you will be at a positional disadvantage to the big blind. This means that with a hand like

you usually should just call. In fact, since you do not have position over the big blind, you should call rather than raise with most of the hands you will be playing heads up against the big blind.

The exception is when the big blind throws away too many hands in this situation. For example, in a $10-$20 game, it costs you $15 to raise when you have the little blind. There is $15 in the pot already. Therefore, if the big blind folds more than 50 percent of the time, you would show an immediate profit with any two cards. Add this to the fact that you sometimes will win when you are called, and it becomes worthwhile to raise when your chances of stealing the ante are as little as 30 percent. Few players in the big blind will discard their hands this often in this situation, but when you find one who will, you should take advantage of him.

The First Two Cards: Late-Position Blind

In most cardrooms, if you miss your blinds or have just entered a game, you are allowed to post what is known as a late-position blind. If you are new to the game, you must post an amount equal to the big blind; if you have missed the blinds, you must post an amount equal to both the big and the little blinds. However, in both cases, only an amount equal to the big blind is live. (This late-position blind is posted in addition to the big and small blinds to the left of the dealer button.)

Because of your improved position and the increased amount of money in the pot, there are some significant strategy changes versus regular blind play. For instance, if everyone passes, you usually should raise, no matter what hand you have. This is one of those situations where either folding or raising is the best play, while just calling is usually the worst option. But because you already have posted your blind, you cannot fold. This means that raising is usually correct. The exception is when you are against opponents who almost always will defend their blinds, no matter how poor their hands are. In this case, it is best to call with some of your weaker hands.

However, if some players already have called, there are few situations where you would raise with a hand that you normally would not raise with (if you did not post a late-position blind). In fact, you may want to raise less often, since your opponents will now misread the strength of your hand.

Because of your position, if the pot is raised in front of you, you can call with a hand slightly worse than what you would play in the big blind. This means that you still must be very selective, especially if you are against a good player. Also, remember to distinguish between a legitimate raise and a possible steal-raise. Against the latter, it is probably OK to call with any ace and most kings, depending on how well your opponent plays.

The First Two Cards
Afterthought

We have seen that in Texas hold'em, it is relatively easy to specify exactly how the first two cards should be played. This is because at this stage of play, the situation is not yet that complicated. This doesn't mean that you cannot make mistakes, but it does mean that if you understand the situation and have good judgment, it should be fairly clear as to what the correct play should be. Unfortunately, as we shall soon see, this is not always true with play on the flop and beyond.

Another thing to keep in mind when playing hold'em is that it is easy to become frustrated and to start playing too many hands. For example, a hand like

can begin to look almost as good as a hand like

In some situations, such as when you are in a steal position and no one has yet entered the pot, this is probably true. But in other spots, having the bigger kicker is crucial. If an ace flops, a queen might win where a ten won't, plus you are much more likely to flop top pair with a queen than with a ten. In addition, if you do flop top pair with a queen than a ten, you don't have to worry as much about overcards hitting on a later round. This sometimes will allow you to play your hand much differently and for much more profit.

These ideas, though detailed, are all very important. But even though playing your first two cards correctly is absolutely crucial to winning play, this will not automatically make you a winner. In fact, perfect play on the first two cards will enable you only to break even at best, assuming that the rest of your game is fairly good.

Part Two

Strategic Concepts

Strategic Concepts

Introduction

Most of the profit in hold'em comes from knowing how to play after the first round. Unfortunately, the game quickly becomes so complex that it is impossible to discuss every situation, which is why it's important to develop general strategic concepts to guide you toward winning play.

That is the purpose of this section. When you finish reading it, you should have a good idea of how to approach most situations at the hold'em table. Although you won't be an expert yet as this additionally requires a great deal of experience, you should be well on your way toward achieving this goal.

Also, at this juncture, we would like to recommend a more general book on poker concepts, namely *The Theory of Poker* by David Sklansky. While not specifically about hold'em, this book is must reading for all serious players.

Semi-Bluffing

In *The Theory of Poker*, David Sklansky defines a semi-bluff as "a bet with a hand which, if called, does not figure to be the best hand at the moment but has a reasonable chance of outdrawing those hands that initially called it." Notice that when you are semi-bluffing, there are two ways that you might win the pot. First, no one may call and you will win the pot immediately. Second, if you do get customers, you still may improve to the best hand. It is the combination of these two possibilities that makes this class of plays profitable, and as we shall see, semi-bluffing plays a crucial role in any winning hold'em strategy. Also notice that the semi-bluff necessarily means that more cards are to come.

Obvious examples of semi-bluff situations in hold'em are when you have flopped an inside straight draw, or second or third pair with an overcard kicker. In these examples, you would prefer that all of your opponents fold. However, if you are called, you still have a chance to win if the right card comes on the turn. A specific example of a semi-bluff situation is when you hold

against not too many opponents, and the flop comes

In this case, an eight will give you the absolute nuts, and a nine or a ten will give you an overpair (to the flop), which also may be good enough to win.

You might not want to semi-bluff when you are in last position. Now the problem with betting is that you may be check-raised, and instead of seeing the next card for free, it will cost you two bets. Often, the factor that determines whether to bet in this situation is how frequently you think you will be check-raised. This is a function of the opponents you are up against. Keep in mind that some players constantly will go for a check-raise, while other players seldom will make this play. (More discussion on this concept appears later in the text.)

However, your bet in this spot also may buy you a free card on a succeeding round, which is another reason to semi-bluff. As usual, experience and a knowledge of how your opponents play will help you make the right decisions in these situations.

Here is another example of a correct semi-bluff. You hold

and the flop is

Notice that you have middle pair with the very best kicker, plus "back-door" flush potential. (Backdoor flush potential means that you will make a flush if both the fourth- and fifth-street cards are of your suit.) The correct play is to bet if you think you have any chance of winning the pot immediately. If you get called, you still can win if an ace or a trey comes on the turn. Against poor players who call too much, semi-bluffing may not be correct in this situation. (Although a bet might be worth it, since you will be called with worse hands.)

Following are some other examples of correct semi-bluffs. First, let's look at a four flush or open-end straight draw — especially with a pair — with one card to come. Suppose you hold

and the board is

Notice that you have a pair, plus a flush draw. This means that there are 14 cards left in the deck (out of the remaining 46 unseen cards) that will give you a strong hand. (If you had an open-end straight draw and a pair, there would be 13 cards left in the deck that would give you a strong hand.) This is usually enough potential, along with the possibility that all of your opponents may fold, to make a bet the correct move. If you do not have a pair — that is, you have only a straight draw (eight outs) or a flush draw (nine outs) — your hand is not as good. However, this does not mean that it is correct to check (and then call if there is a bet), but that you should bet only if you think there is a decent chance that all of your opponents will fold.

Let's look at the small pair with an overcard kicker. Suppose you have

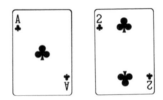

the flop is

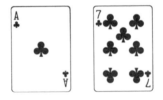

and there are six people in the pot. It is still correct to bet against typical players. However, it would be different if you had

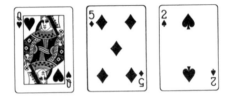

and the flop came

There is a good chance that other players would like this flop, as straight draws are now likely. In addition, if the flop comes with two suited cards, be less inclined to semi-bluff, especially against a lot of opponents, since a flush draw will surely play against you.

Now suppose the flop is

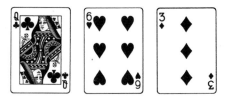

and you hold

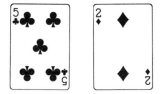

(giving you a "gut shot") against many opponents. This is another time when semi-bluffing is usually correct. However, if the flop comes

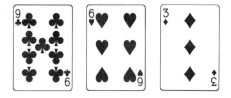

and you hold the same 5♣2♦, it is probably best not to semi-bluff, because with a nine-high flop, it is easy for two overcards to call. However, with a queen-high flop, an opponent must have precisely AK to have two overcards. That is, in the second example, it is much harder to win by betting, thus making a semi-bluff incorrect. (Another reason not to bet is that a four may make a higher straight for someone else.)

Here is a good rule to follow: If your hand is worth a call or even almost worth a call if you check, then it is better to bet if there is some chance that you can win the pot right there. Notice that we are not mentioning the fear of a raise on the flop, as the threat of a raise does not automatically stop us from semi-bluffing. This is because in today's structure, the bet on the flop is often very small when compared with the size of the pot. Of course, if you think there is a good possibility of being raised, then this is another matter. The criterion of having some chance of winning the pot immediately is diminished, and it would have been incorrect to semi-bluff to begin with.

A secondary advantage to semi-bluffing is that when you do make your hand, your opponent often will misread it. Suppose in the gut-shot draw example, you have 5♣2♦ and the flop is Q♣6♥3♦. Now a four comes on the next card. Who would dream that you have made a straight? If it turns out that you happen to be up against another strong hand, such as a set of sixes, you might get almost unlimited action.

A third advantage to semi-bluffing is that it keeps your opponents guessing. If you never bluff, you are simply giving away too much information. Players in this category are referred to as "weak tight." They are easy to make money against, since you virtually always know exactly where they are, but they have a great deal of trouble figuring out what your hand is. Semi-bluffing is a good way to mix up your play so you can't be "read" as easily.

And finally, a fourth advantage of semi-bluffing, as we mentioned earlier, is that you may get a free card on the next round. This is especially true against timid players, who are afraid to bet into anyone who has shown strength.

One last situation that we would like to address in this section is how to play two overcards on the flop. Overcards frequently should be bet, especially if you have back-door flush potential, unless you think a reasonable chance exists that if you catch your card, you still won't win. Thus if a straight-type flop hits, or a flop with two suited cards, you would be less inclined to bet, especially against many opponents.

If you do bet two overcards and are raised, the question now is whether you should call. The answer, again, depends on what you think your chances of winning are if one of your overcards hits and on the pot odds you are getting. This is another spot where good judgment, experience, and knowledge of your opponent can help in determining your decision.

Finally, if someone else bets on the flop, is it correct to call with two overcards? This also relates to your judgment concerning your chances of winning if one of your overcards hits and to your pot odds. Look at the texture of the flop. Specifically, be more inclined to call with a flop like

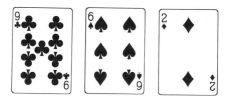

than with a flop like

Notice that with the second flop, you are more likely to be against two pair, as the typical player will enter a pot more often with a hand like

than with a hand like

And if you do decide that your hand (two overcards) is worth playing (usually because of the chances that you will improve, plus the chances that you have the best hand), you should consider *raising* rather than calling. If nothing else, this play may get you a free card — a subject that is covered in the next chapter.

The Free Card

When you bet or raise on an early round in order to get checked to on the next round, you are not actually getting a free card. In reality, you are getting a card cheaply. If everything works, it appears as though you are getting a free card, but that "free" card cost you a bet on the previous round. If things do not work as hoped, the free card you are trying to get may become quite expensive. (Your opponent might reraise.) However, there are many situations where trying for a free card is beneficial.

Since getting a free card is often advantageous when your hand is weak, it should be obvious that when you have a legitimate hand, it is usually to your disadvantage to give any free cards. Specifically, you should bet most of your legitimate hands to give your opponent a chance to drop. This includes holdings like four flushes or open-end straight draws with two cards to come. By the way, be willing to bet open-end straight draws with two flush cards on board, as long as there are still two cards to come. It is true that you may make your straight and run into a flush. But notice that it is often correct to bet on the flop with a small pair and an overcard, a hand that has only five cards that will improve it. Even if a flush draw is out, you still have six cards that will make your straight draw a winning hand, and many times that winning hand will be the "nuts."

You also usually should bet top pair or an overpair on the flop, as long as your hand figures to be the best hand. The exceptions are when there is a lot of raising before the flop, indicating that you may not have the best hand, and those times when you have decided to check-raise. (These topics are discussed in more detail later in the text.) Specifically, resist the inclination to check to the before-the-flop-raiser. Checking and calling is rarely a correct strategy in hold'em, yet this is precisely the way that many weak opponents will play.

However, there are three situations where checking and calling may be correct. The first occurs when you are slow-playing. (This topic is addressed later in the text.) The second situation is when you are fairly sure that your opponent has a better hand and will not fold if you bet, but the pot odds justify your calling in the hope that either you have the best hand or you may outdraw your opponent. The third situation is when you arc against a habitual bluffer. Now, even though you risk giving a free card, checking and calling is probably the best strategy to follow.

Another interesting concept is that even when you are a big favorite and want callers, but you think everyone will fold if you bet, giving a free card still may be incorrect. In this case, the next card might be a miracle card for someone else, but it is not likely to make anyone a second-best hand. An obvious example of this can be seen when you flop a small flush. A check could give someone else a higher flush, and that person would not have called your bet. Specifically, suppose you hold

and three spades flop. If you bet, someone with the 8♠, 9♠, T♠, or J♠ most likely will throw his hand away. If you check and a fourth spade comes, you may have cost yourself the pot.

These examples illustrate the general principle of free cards. That is, if you check and allow someone who would not have called your bet to outdraw you, then you have allowed a "mathematical catastrophe" to happen. It is also a catastrophe to give a free card to someone who would have called your bet, and he fails to outdraw you. However, this second mathematical catastrophe is not as bad as the first.

There are four other basic situations where it is correct to check on the flop. The first is when you are sure that you do not have the best hand and especially sure that you will be called if you bet. This frequently will occur when you have several opponents and the board flops either three cards that rank close to each other or two suited cards.

For instance, suppose you have

you are against several opponents, and the flop is

It is usually wrong to bet. There is little chance that everyone will fold, and you have almost no chance of improving to the best hand.

The second situation where it is generally correct to check is when you think it is likely that someone behind you will bet. This often occurs when you are in a two-person pot and were raised by a very aggressive opponent before the flop. Some of these players automatically will bet on the flop when you check to them, no matter which cards have come.

When this is the case and you have flopped a strong hand, almost always go for a check-raise. In fact, with a non-threatening flop, you sometimes should check-raise and then bet again on fourth street even when you have nothing. (However, don't get carried away with this play. Make it only occasionally.)

The third situation where it is correct to check is with a hand that should be slow-played. As already noted, this will be covered later in the text.

Finally, when you have flopped top pair, either aces or kings, and you have a weak kicker it might be right to check and call. Notice that if you don't have the best hand, you save money by not having to call any raise. Also notice (and this is extremely important) that few free cards can hurt you. Specifically, when you have aces and, to a lesser degree, kings, you are not worried about overcards beating you.

But suppose you have flopped top pair, not aces or kings, and you have a weak kicker. This usually happens when you get a "free" play in the big blind. How should this hand be played?

The answer is somewhat complex. Against a small number of opponents, you should bet so you are not giving a free card that could easily beat you. Against a large number of opponents, you should check and perhaps fold if it is bet early and you have players behind you. This is because with several players still to act, it is unlikely that the bettor would bet a hand that you could beat. (The pot is said to be "protected.") Few players will bluff in this spot. Though your opponent may be betting a draw, the combination of factors should deter you from calling, unless the pot is offering very good odds.

But if the bet comes from a late-position player after you have checked to a large number of opponents, you should raise. Even though you don't have to hold the best hand, there is a good chance that you do, and by getting the pot heads-up, you will maximize your chances of winning.

Here's an example. Suppose the flop is

No one raised before the flop, many players are in the pot, and you are in the blind with a queen and a weak kicker. You should check, and if a late-position player bets, you should raise (regardless of your kicker.) You are trying to restrict the competition to a small number of players, most likely just you and the bettor, and since there were few players behind the late-position bettor, a good chance exists that you have the best hand.

However, you must be cautious if you have top pair (with a weak kicker) that is below queens. This is especially true against tough players for a little-known reason that normally is considered only by experts.

The principle is that it is more probable for someone else to have top pair in an unraised pot when the top card is a jack or lower. This is because good players are more likely either to raise or fold when they have an ace, king, or queen in their hands (depending on their other card) and less likely to just call. Thus, when nobody raises before the flop, a flop like

is not likely to make a pair of kings for someone else. So if you played

in the blind, you should like your hand. However, if you hold

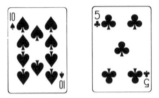

and the flop is

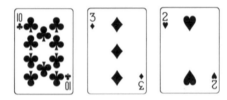

you must fear the possibility of a ten — unraised pot or not —
since most players will just call with a hand like

or

In this case, unless you have a good kicker, or the pot is quite
large, or you have a back-door flush draw, you usually should
fold top pair with no kicker when that top pair is jacks or lower.
(However, if you do play, you generally should raise.)

One concept that we already have stressed is to avoid
checking to the before-the-flop raiser in most situations. But

many players do this. So if you are the before-the-flop raiser in a multiway pot, your hand is weak, and everyone checks to you, you almost always should take a free card. But under the same circumstances in a short-handed pot, you should bet, especially if you think there is a reasonable chance that you can win the pot right there.

Following is a slightly different example of this concept. Suppose you hold

the flop is

and everyone checks to you. If the pot is being played short-handed, you should bet. The main reason for this is that you don't want to give a free card to someone holding a hand like

This bet also might gain you a free card on the next round. In fact, betting or raising in late position with a hand that does not seem to justify it is sometimes correct if you think this may gain you a free card. However, keep in mind that if you take

the free card, some opponents automatically will bet on the river, no matter what they have or what the last card is. Against these types of players, it is frequently necessary to call with as little as ace high after you have shown weakness by checking on fourth street.

A somewhat related example is to raise in late position on the flop with a four flush. If the game is not tough — that is, you do not fear a reraise and your raise will encourage your opponents to check to you on the next round — you should raise more than half the time. However, you want players with this type of flop. Consequently, if there is a bet and several players remain to act behind you, it is often better to just call. (You still should consider raising if the pot is large, especially if you have overcards.)

Incidentally, even if you can't get a free card with your flush draw, since the odds against making your hand are approximately 2-to-1, your raise is also correct if you are sure that at least three players will call. An exception occurs if a pair flopped. In this case, you can make your flush and still lose the pot, so you usually should just call. This concept is discussed in more detail later in the text.

Keep in mind that any time you are in a late position on the flop and have a hand that is worth a call, you should seriously consider raising. In fact, sometimes it is worth raising when you are absolutely sure that the bettor has you beat.

Here is an example. Suppose that five players have put in three bets each before the flop. You are in last position with

and are sure that no one has aces or kings, since you put in the last raise. The flop is

If the player to your right bets after everyone else has checked, you should raise, even if you are sure that he has two tens. Since the pot has become very large, it is important that you maximize your chances of winning it, even if you cost yourself a few more bets. In the example given, your raise on the flop probably has increased your chances from about 15 percent (had you just called) to about 25 percent. By knocking people out, you have made it more likely that you will win if a queen or a jack comes. Though this play may cost you more money, it is well worth it. Additionally, it may *save* you money if your raise has scared the bettor into just calling and then checking on fourth street. As far as your back-door flush and straight chances are concerned, you probably would win with these hands, even if you let everybody in. However, the extra back-door chances are what made it wrong to fold originally, and as we've just shown, if you don't fold, it is better to raise.

Here is another example of how back-door potential can improve your hand and make a raise correct. Suppose you have

and the flop is

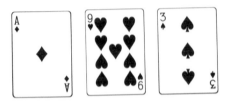

Notice that the flop includes an ace and one of your suit. If someone else bets, you should raise. Now bet on the turn with the intention of just showing down on the river if you do not improve. If you get check-raised on fourth street, you usually should fold, unless you helped or picked up a flush draw. You don't have enough chance to draw out against a legitimate hand to make it worth calling the check-raise. But if your opponent may be bluffing or semi-bluffing, you've got to keep him honest. Had you not flopped a three flush with your pair of aces, a raise on the flop is less likely to be correct. In fact, without the back-door flush potential, it may be better to fold.

Slow-Playing

Slow-playing basically means to play a hand weakly on one round of betting in order to lure people in for later bets. Hands that are correct to slow-play don't come up very often. For a slow-play to be correct the following criteria must be met:

1. Your hand must be very strong.
2. You probably will chase everyone out by betting, but you have a good chance of winning a large pot if you check.
3. The free card that you are giving has good possibilities of making second-best hands.
4. This free card has little chance of making a better hand for someone or even of giving him a draw to a better hand with sufficient odds to justify a call.
5. The pot must not yet be very large.

An example of a correct slow-play is to check a set of jacks when the flop comes

Notice that in this example, an overcard on fourth street can easily give someone a second-best hand. Conversely, with a lot of opponents, someone could pick up a flush draw or an open-end straight draw on the turn and could then beat you on the end. So even here, slow-playing may not be correct if the pot has become large (or if several bad players, who may call your bet with as little as one overcard, are in the pot.)

Keep in mind that if the situation is not perfect, slow-playing is almost never correct. For example, if the flop is

and you have

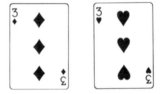

you usually should bet or raise on the flop, as your opponents can hold many possible hands, including flush and straight draws.

Another time that you generally should not slow-play is when you have flopped the absolute nuts. This is because an opponent also may have flopped a very strong hand and will give you plenty of action. For instance, don't slow-play the nut flush if there is a chance that someone else also may have flopped a flush. If he is slow-playing, you will have cost yourself a lot of money.

In addition, remember that for slow-playing to be correct, your opponents must have the opportunity to make a good second-best hand. As an example, if you hold two aces and a third ace flops, it is generally correct to bet and pick up the pot. In this case, there is usually not a second-best hand for your opponents to make, but a miracle card could cause you to lose the pot.

A strategy similar to slow-playing is to just call someone else's bet in order to reraise a raiser behind you or to go for a raise on fourth street when the bet is twice as large. To do this, your hand must be almost as strong as a regular slow-playing hand.

For instance, when you flop top two pair and the player on your immediate right bets into you, you may want to wait until the turn to raise. That is, just call on the flop. This play is optimal if you are sure that this player will bet again. However, should a third player raise behind you, it is probably better to reraise on the flop and gain extra bets from all your opponents.

Here's an example. Suppose you limp in with

you are raised by an aggressive player behind you, and a player in the blind calls. Now suppose the flop is

and the player in the blind leads out. You should just call with the intention of raising him on fourth street. However, if the original raiser now raises behind you, you usually should go ahead and reraise. This would be especially true if this opponent is the type of player who would raise with a hand like

in the hope of getting a free card.

Check-Raising

Check-raising is the play of checking your hand with the intention of raising on the same round after an opponent bets. Notice that check-raising and slow-playing are two ways of playing a strong hand weakly to trap your opponents. However, they are not the same thing. In addition, the check-raise often has the ability to exclude opponents from competing for the pot. Sometimes, in limit hold'em, this is the most desirable characteristic of check-raising.

For check-raising to be correct, you usually should (1) think you have the best hand and (2) be quite sure that someone will bet behind you if you check. A situation where check-raising probably would be correct is when you flop two pair and there are many players on the flop.

Sometimes it is also correct to check-raise with a drawing hand. An example is when you think a player to your left will bet and two or more players will call. However, don't raise if you fear a reraise or if a reasonable chance exists that your hand won't win even if you hit it (perhaps a pair shows). Also keep in mind that a four flush or an open-end straight draw normally should just be bet if there is any chance that you can steal the pot.

Two other interesting things may happen if you check a lot of good hands on the flop. First, some of your opponents may become afraid to bet. That is, they may be more inclined to give you a free card, and this free card may win the pot for you. Second, even if a blank hits on the turn, you now may be able to steal the pot. Your opponents are not going to suspect a bluff merely because you didn't bet on the flop as they know you might have been trying for a check-raise. In fact, some of your opponents might feel smug when you bet, since they "escaped your trap." (When you are bluffing in this situation, never show your hand.) However, remember that if you check a lot of hands on the flop, the free card that you give occasionally may cost you the pot.

You also can check-raise semi-bluff. For example, suppose you have

and the flop comes

You bet and are raised, and you (correctly) call the raise. The next card is the

Now the correct play is for you to check-raise. You want your opponent to fold, but with your straight-flush draw, you have a lot of outs even if you are called.

Here is another example. Suppose you hold

and the flop comes

If any spade hits on fourth street, you can try for a check-raise. This is probably the right play whether or not you were raised on the flop.

There is another very important reason to check-raise, and in many situations, it should be the dominant factor that you consider. It is the fact that in games of today's structure, the bet on the flop is often not large enough, when compared to the size of the pot, to make it incorrect for drawing hands (and this includes hands like middle pair) to call. This means that you should check-raise a fair amount of time in an attempt to cut down the odds for opponents to draw out on you. A good guideline to follow is to consider check-raising if it is unlikely that an overcard can hurt you. That is, if you flop top pair and your top pair is aces, kings, or queens (and you have an overcard kicker with your queen), check-raising is often the correct play, especially if several players remain to act behind you. If your top pair is lower than queens, it is more dangerous to try for a check-raise, since a free card can easily beat you.

However, if you have top pair in a large multiway pot, even if you are afraid of an overcard, it still may be correct to check-raise, especially if you are in an early position. This is because the pot is now so large that if you bet, you can expect a lot of callers anyway. Consequently, in an effort to thin the field, it may be necessary to risk the dreaded free card.

Here's an example. You are in an early position and hold

in a multiway pot. The flop comes

You must consider going for a check-raise. If you bet into many players and the pot is large, you probably will get several callers, and an ace or a king is likely to beat you. But if you go for a check-raise and are able to isolate a late-position player, you still may win if one of these cards hits. Your check-raise also is likely to force out hands such as 87, while a simple bet wouldn't. Now you've eliminated the 1-in-5 chance that a player holding this type of hand will beat you.

Odds and Implied Odds

Most players make many of their calling decisions based on the size of the pot related to the current bet. While this does give an indication of what is correct, pot odds should be adjusted based on the expected future action of your opponents. For example, if the bettor is to your right and there are other players who might raise behind you, you should adjust the pot odds considerably lower. Specifically, you would reduce your calling frequency, since there is a possibility of a raise behind you.

Here are two extreme examples of this concept. First, suppose you hold

and the flop is

You should fold if you are in second position, a solid player to your right bets, a number of players are behind you, and there has been no raise before the flop.

A second example is to fold in the same situation if you hold

and the flop is

Exceptions to folding these hands are when the pot has become very large and/or the game is very loose. (The first condition is often the case in today's games, but don't use this as an excuse to make an automatic call.) Also, remember that calling is sometimes the worst play. That is, folding or raising in these situations is usually a superior strategy. If the pot is large and you are going to play, it is generally correct to raise with these types of hands. You should seldom call as you cannot afford to give someone behind you who holds a marginal hand the correct odds to draw out on you.

In addition, if you call on the flop and intend to also call on fourth street, keep in mind that the pot odds you are getting are not as good as they appear. The additional call that you plan to make lowers the effective odds that you are receiving from the pot. (For a more detailed discussion of these concepts, see *The Theory of Poker* by David Sklansky.)

Sometimes, however, the opposite will be the case. That is, your implied odds actually are better than the odds that the pot is offering you. This occurs when you plan to continue playing only if you hit your hand. Otherwise, you will fold. What this means is that the pot does not have to offer you seemingly correct odds to play a particular hand.

An example is to call before the flop with a small pair, if there is little danger of a raise, when you have odds of only about 5-to-1. (The odds against flopping a set are approximately 7½-to-1.) A second example is to try for an inside straight on the flop when you have odds of only about 8-to-1. (The odds against making your gut shot are approximately 11-to-1.) By the way, in a loose passive game, where you anticipate a lot of callers, small pairs can be played up front even if you do not have odds (as yet) as good as 5-to-1.

Specifically, if you hold

and the flop is

you can call even if you are getting a little less than the required 11-to-1. However, if a two flush is on board, or for some other reason you are not sure that your hand will be good if you hit it, you probably would want odds of at least 11-to-1 to call.

Finally, even if the odds don't seem to justify it, you still should make a loose call every now and then, as you don't want to become known as a "folder." If you are regarded as a folder, other players will try to run over you, and otherwise predictable opponents may turn tricky and become difficult to play against. (Once again, for a more thorough analysis of pot odds and implied odds, see *The Theory of Poker* by David Sklansky.)

Bluffing

Bluffing is the act of betting when you are quite sure that you do not have the best hand and you have little chance of making the best hand. When you bluff, you are hoping that your opponent will fold. Typically, you should bluff when you think the size of the pot, compared to the estimated probability that your opponent will fold, is large enough to make this play profitable (in terms of long-run expectation). For example, if there is $50 in the pot and the bet is $10, you are getting 5-to-1 odds on your bluff. In this situation, if you think your opponent will fold more than one time in six, then bluffing certainly would be correct.

Sometimes you should bluff even if the pot odds do not justify it, as this makes it more difficult for your opponent to read your hands in the future. (While this is an excellent play against a good player, an expert player probably will be perceptive enough to understand what you are doing.)

Here is an example of a good fifth-street bluff. Suppose that you have only one opponent remaining, you are trying for a straight, and a third suited card appears on board. Against a player who is capable of folding, you may want to attempt a bluff. Specifically, suppose you started with

and on fifth street, the board is

Whether you have been betting or calling up to this point, you should now consider betting if you are against a player who is capable of folding.

Sometimes the situation arises when you have very little but still may have the best hand. Rather than check, it may be more beneficial to bet, just in case your bet makes an opponent fold a better hand. Occasionally this play works even more to your advantage when someone holding a worse hand calls. In a multiway pot, you may accomplish both objectives, which is the best result of all. As an example, suppose you are in an early position against a small number of players. Everyone checks on the flop and on fourth street. The board now pairs on fifth street, and you have a small pair or a hand like

In this situation it is unlikely that the fifth-street card helped anyone. So if you bet and are called, you still may win the pot. Meanwhile, you may have forced someone else to fold a better hand.

An obvious example of a fourth-street bluff occurs when you are in a late position and everyone has checked on both the flop and fourth street. Now there is a good chance that a bet will win the pot right there, no matter what you have.

A good bluffing opportunity also arises on the flop in short-handed pots when no one has shown any strength. Suppose that you are in an early position — perhaps you were given a free play in the big blind — and the flop comes either ace high or king high with no flush or straight opportunities for drawing hands. A bet here should steal the pot often enough to make it profitable. This is especially true if, as already mentioned, you are in a game where most players tend to raise with better hands containing an ace or a king, and to throw away the other ace and king hands.

Specifically, flops like

are excellent candidates for this type of bluff. Remember, you want to be in early position, and you want the pot to be small.

Finally, a word must be said about when you should call an opponent who might be bluffing. If all the cards are out and your hand can beat only a bluff, your decision simply depends on your pot odds and on your judgment concerning the chances that your opponent is bluffing. But you don't need as good pot odds if your hand can beat some of the hands he would bet for value, as well as his bluffs.

Inducing Bluffs

The ability to induce bluffs is a sign of expert play. The idea is to manipulate your opponent into betting a hand that he originally had no intention of betting. These situations usually occur when you have a good calling hand. Consequently, since you plan to call anyway, you want to make sure that your opponent bets as often as possible those times when you likely hold the better hand.

Usually, these plays are accomplished by making what seems to be an otherwise irrational check, and they work best when you are against an aggressive player. A well-known example occurs when you hold either AA or KK and raise in last position before the flop. Now suppose the flop comes with a medium or small pair, it is checked to you, you bet, and a tough player calls. On fourth street, the correct play is to check behind your opponent if he checks again. Notice that if he has flopped a set, your check probably will save you money. But, if he has no pair, you may get him to bluff at the pot on the end. The result is that you have gained an extra bet, since he likely would not have called your bet on the turn. (By the way, you never would make this play with a hand like JJ, since too many overcards that could beat you might hit on the end.)

Before inducing a bluff, several criteria have to be met. First, you usually should be facing only a small number of opponents, preferably just one. Second, you need to be against a player who is capable of bluffing but also capable of folding if you bet. This is why you want for your opponent to be the tough but aggressive type. And finally, as already pointed out in the example just given, the situation must be such that giving a free card to your opponent is not dangerous if his hand is worse than yours.

Here is a second example of this type of play. Suppose you hold and raise from a late position. You are reraised by the player in the big blind, and the flop comes

Your opponent bets and you call. On fourth street, a blank hits and your opponent checks. You also should check with the intention of betting or calling on the river. Notice that if your opponent has a better hand than you have, you avoid being check-raised. Consequently, if your opponent cannot beat an ace, there is a good chance that he will either bet or call on the river when he might have folded on fourth street if you had bet your hand.

A third example is somewhat different, because it requires a multiway pot. Suppose you are in a late position, against several opponents. A fourth suited card hits on the turn, you have the king of that suit, and everyone has checked to you. The correct play may be for you to also check. If you bet, you may not get any calls, plus if the ace of the appropriate suit is in one of your opponents' hands, you save money. However, by checking, you may induce a bluff, and if you don't induce a bluff, someone who would not have called on the turn may now call on the river.

For example, suppose you hold

in a multiway pot, and you are on the button. The flop comes

and the turn card is the

If no one bets, strongly consider checking. If someone bets on fifth street, always call; if it is checked to you on fifth street, always bet; and if you now get checked-raised, always call. Remember, your check on fourth street may encourage someone to take a shot at you when you bet on the river.

Finally, we want to remind you once again that a fuller treatment of both bluffing and inducing bluffs can be found in *The Theory of Poker* by David Sklansky.

Folding When the Pot is Big

In hold'em, situations sometimes develop where it is virtually impossible for your opponent to be bluffing. This is due to the community cards that are present in this game. Consequently, even though the pot may be quite large, it is frequently correct to throw away your hand.

As an example, suppose the pot is many-handed and you get a free play in the big blind. You hold

and the flop comes

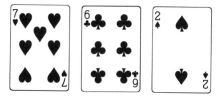

You check, planning to check-raise, but no one bets. The fourth-street card is the

Again you check, planning to check-raise. But this time, one player bets and another calls and then you check raise, limiting the pot to just the three of you. On fifth street, another queen hits. Even though the pot is large, the correct play now is to check and fold, since at least one of your opponents will always have you beaten — probably by three queens.

Heads-up Versus Multiway

Keep in mind that many of the fancy plays we have been talking about do not work well when you are against a lot of opponents. In fact, making some of these plays in multiway pots will cost you money in the long run. Specifically, against many opponents, you should slow-play less, if at all, semi-bluff less, avoid bluffing — especially on the end against more than two opponents — and avoid inducing bluffs.

However, with many players in the pot, your implied odds usually have increased. This means that you are much more apt to play and even raise with small pairs, suited connectors, and hands like

On the other hand, when you hold big unsuited cards, your opponents are getting implied odds from you. Therefore, it is wrong to raise with unsuited high cards in multiway pots, and it may be right to fold hands like AT, KT, and even AJ and KJ.

Specifically, if you hold

on the button, and five or six players have limped in, you should strongly consider folding. Raising with this hand — which is a mistake frequently made by beginning players — will cost you money in the long run. Even calling might be wrong for all but the best players.

Raising

There are five basic reasons to raise in hold'em:

1. To get more money in the pot.
2. To drive players out.
3. To bluff (or semi-bluff).
4. To get a free card.
5. To gain information.

If you think you have the bettor beat, it is generally correct to raise, even if you risk driving out players behind you. In fact, in most cases, it is very important to drive out players on the flop. This is because in today's modern structure, the size of the pot is often so large in relation to the bet on the flop that it sometimes becomes correct to draw to long-shot hands if there is no raise (on the flop). Consequently, your raise in these spots often will save the whole pot for you.

By the way, if you are raising on the flop to drive people out, it usually will work only against those players who have not yet had a chance to call the original bet. It is a rare player who will fold his hand on the flop for one more bet after he already has put money into the pot. (Sometimes, however, the original bettor will help you drive out players by reraising.)

Even if you are not sure that you have the best hand, a raise is often correct. However, always keep in mind that if you do hold the best hand, or if your hand becomes the best hand, your raise may have stopped other opponents from drawing out on you.

Here is an example of raising with a probable second-best hand. Suppose you raised before the flop with

and the flop is

Notice that you have a pair and an overcard, plus back-door straight and back-door flush potential. If someone on your right bets, a raise is often correct, especially if you think that the raise will buy you a free card.

In very tough games, raising as a pure bluff can be done occasionally, because players are capable of folding in big pots without calling one last bet. An example of this type of play is when one player bets and another calls on the river. If the right cards are out — especially if a scare card that is unlikely to help either of your opponents hits on the river — you can raise. This raise often works against the right players since there is also a caller, who obviously is not bluffing. Thus it looks as though you have something.

However, these plays usually are not recommended, simply because they succeed rarely and are expensive when they fail. However, if the conditions are perfect and you know your opponents well, you occasionally may find an opportunity to pull this play off successfully.

By the way, the one time that you can bluff-raise in a weaker game is when you think your opponent is bluffing but also think your hand is even worse. An example is when your flush draw did not get there, but the hand was played in such a fashion that you are fairly sure your opponent was also on a flush draw.

Here's an example of this play. Suppose you start with

and the flop is

An opponent bets, you just call, your opponent does not have a history of trying to check-raise, and just the two of you are in the pot. A blank hits on fourth street, and both you and your opponent check. Notice that there is a good chance that he is also on a flush draw and was betting on the flop in an attempt to pick up the pot. If another blank hits on the river and he bets, you may want to raise. If he was just on a flush draw, a good chance exists that you will win the pot.

You also can raise as a semi-bluff. For example, suppose you have

the flop is

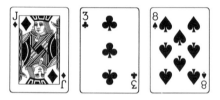

and everyone checks. If the next card is the

giving you the nut flush draw and a gut-shot straight draw, you should raise if someone bets.

A similar opportunity to raise sometimes occurs in a short-handed pot when everyone checks on the flop and fourth street does not bring an overcard or three to a straight or flush, but it gives you either a flush draw or an open-end straight draw. Now suppose an early-position player bets, and you know it is likely that he would try to steal in this spot. Your correct play is to raise in the hope that your opponent will fold. But if he does not fold, you still have some outs.

Here's an example of this play. You start with

and the flop is

No one bets, and the turn card is the

giving you an open-end straight draw. If an early-position player bets, and he is the type of player who would try to pick up the pot with no hand, you should go ahead and raise. If he calls with a legitimate hand, you still have at least eight outs to win.

An opportunity for a semi-bluff raise also occurs almost any time that you pick up a back-door flush draw after calling on the flop with a pair. But again, make this play only against someone who you think is capable of folding.

This brings up another concept. That is, how likely it is that someone will fold. This is based on the answers to three questions. First, how capable is this person of folding a big hand? Second, how likely is he to be semi-bluffing? (Of course, this is a matter of watching your opponent and learning exactly how he plays.) And third, how are you perceived by this particular individual? Specifically, if other players think you virtually never bluff, you are more likely to get away with this play than if they think you are a wild and reckless player.

Raising to get a free card is best done when you are in late position and the bet is smaller than the bets on succeeding rounds. Moreover, any hand that is worth a call is conceivably worth a raise.

Finally, raising to gain information should be done only rarely, usually just in heads-up situations. Even in the most favorable spots, this raise probably is not worth it, as you usually have to "pay" too much for the information. However, if your hand may be worth a raise anyway, the fact that you will gain information (based on how your opponent responds to your raise) might make raising the right play.

Heads-up on Fifth Street

Many pots in hold'em, even though they may start with a lot of players, often end up as two-player contests by the time all the cards are out. Consequently, on the end, you sometimes must apply concepts that are totally different from those that were operative in earlier betting rounds. This section provides some guidelines on how to proceed. First, let's discuss those situations where you are last to act.

The first question that many players ask is when is it correct to bluff? The answer is that if your hand probably can't win by checking and the odds you are getting from the pot compared to the chances your opponent will call are favorable, then a bluff will be profitable.

This concept was addressed in an earlier section, so we won't go into detail again. But a lot depends on whether you have been the bettor or the caller. If you have been calling all the way, a significant card that does not help you, such as a flush card on fifth street, may make a bluff correct. If you have been betting all the way, you might try a bluff on the end regardless of the last card. Also, as has been emphasized in the text, remember to consider whether your opponent is capable of folding a decent hand.

One mistake that inexperienced players make is to bet when all the cards are out, simply because they think they have the best hand. The trouble with this play is that while you may have the best hand the majority of the time, your bet may still be a loser. That is, *when you are called*, your bet will lose the majority of the time — even though you expect to have the winning hand in a showdown. In fact, if your opponent has already checked, you should think you have the best hand at least 55 percent of the time *that you are called* for your bet to be correct (51 percent is not good enough because of the possibility that you will be check-raised).

Here are a couple of examples. First, suppose you have

and are against one opponent. The flop comes queen high, with or without two suited cards. If two blanks hit and the action has not been too heavy, you should bet on the river. It is very likely that a lesser hand will call you.

As a second example, suppose everything is the same as before except that the river card pairs the queen. If it is checked to you, a bet is now more dangerous but probably still correct. If the last queen is of the appropriate suit, meaning that a flush draw is now complete, then a bet would be wrong, even though you still have a reasonable chance to win the pot. A bet in this situation is wrong not only because you are less likely to win, but also because you are less likely to be called by a worse hand.

Specifically, if the board on fifth street is

you normally should not bet. Although you still may have the best hand, if you are called, it is unlikely that your hand is good. (If your opponent has come out betting, you should call only if your chances compare favorably with the pot odds. This is often a function of knowing your opponent well and having lots of playing experience.)

Now here is an example of when a call is almost always correct. Suppose you have top pair, you have been betting all the way after your opponent has checked to you on each round, and the lowest card on board pairs on the river. Suddenly, to your surprise, your opponent bets. The question you must ask yourself is this: What could your opponent have been calling with? Is bottom pair a likely candidate? If it is reasonably possible that your opponent has bottom pair, why wouldn't he try to check-raise you on the end when this seemingly innocent card hit? Notice that there is clearly enough doubt in this situation that when the size of the bet is compared to the size of the pot, a call is usually the correct play against all but the most predictable opponents.

When you are planning to raise, you usually need to be about a 2-to-1 favorite on the end (except for bluff-raises) because of the possibility that you may be reraised and the fact that you might not get called unless you are beat. A raise also is generally correct when you think you will have the best hand 55 percent of the time that your raise is called.

When you are first to act, you should always keep in mind what options you have in heads-up, last bet situations. These options are:

1. To bet.
2. To check with the intention of folding.
3. To check with the intention of calling.
4. To check with the intention of raising.

When you have a good hand, whether to check-raise or come right out betting depends on three probabilities: first, the chances that you will be called if you bet, assuming that you won't be raised; second, the chances that your opponent will bet if you check but will not call your raise; and third, the chances that he will bet and then call your raise. Going for a check-raise becomes the correct strategy if the second probability added to twice the third probability exceeds the first probability. Needless to say, this is one of those situations where good judgment will come into play, as you will not have the time to make the appropriate probability calculations at the table.

However, here are some hints that should help you determine whether a check-raise is correct. First, look at the texture of the board. If the river card is likely to give someone a second-best hand that he might believe is the best hand, be more inclined to check. An example is when an ace hits on the end after you have flopped a set, and from the way the hand has been played, you think your opponent called on both the flop and the turn with two overcards.

Second, consider your opponent. Is he the type of player who would always try to pick up the pot if you check but would not be likely to call with a weak hand if you bet? Third, consider whether your opponent is afraid of being check-raised. If he is, then checking to him may be a mistake.

And fourth, consider your previous play in the game. Specifically, if you have done some check-raising, be more inclined to bet out. On the other hand, if you have not been check-raising, now may be the time to try it. Remember, in hold'em, it is important to mix up your play a bit in order to throw your opponents off. However, as we previously have stated, don't mix up your play too much. You have to do it only occasionally to achieve the desired effect.

As far as a check-raise bluff is concerned, it normally will work only against rare opponents in rare situations. Even against good players, it is usually better to come right out betting than to try for a check-raise bluff. The one good time to consider this play is when you have checked a mediocre hand in the hopes of winning a showdown. If your opponent now bets with a hand that you think is only slightly better than yours, a check-raise bluff may be a profitable play.

Here's an example. Suppose you start with

and the flop comes

Notice that your holding is now mediocre, as the flop contains an ace. You bet on both the flop and the turn and are called by an obvious-playing opponent, which makes you think he has an ace but is afraid of his kicker. You also think that if you bet on the river, your opponent will call with his ace. Therefore, you should not bet. But if your opponent bets, he might be susceptible to a check-raise bluff. This doesn't mean that you should go ahead and raise. But this is definitely one of those times that you should consider doing so.

There is also a time when the best strategy is to check and call. This occurs when your opponent will bet with any of the hands that he will call with, plus with some hands that are worse (usually bluffs).

An example of this is against an aggressive opponent who has just been calling after two suited cards appeared on the flop, and you are betting top pair. This opponent may have either middle pair, which he did not think was strong enough to raise with (on the flop), or a flush draw. (Your opponent may not have raised with the flush draw in hopes of getting a free card, because he figured that you were likely to reraise if you indeed have a legitimate hand.) Notice that if your opponent is on a flush draw and the flush card does not get there, he might attempt to bluff if you check. In addition, an aggressive player often will bet middle pair for value. Consequently, in this situation, a check is frequently correct regardless of the last card.

A check in this spot also will eliminate the possibility of a raise. This is especially beneficial when your opponent has middle pair and the last card, which appears to be a blank, may have given him two pair. When this is the case, he often will raise if you bet, especially if the board is not too threatening.

However, against an opponent who will call your bet more often than he will bet himself, you should bet. This is correct even if you are an underdog when he calls, as long as you were going to call his bet anyway, or when folding would be a close decision if you check and he bets. In the previous example, you would bet if, instead of an aggressive opponent, you were up against someone who was fairly timid and would not bet middle pair but would call with this hand. By the way, in this situation it may appear as though the 55 percent rule has been violated, but this rule applies only when you are second to act and your opponent has already checked.

Here is another example. Suppose you have

and when all the cards are out, the board is

Notice that when you bet, you could lose to a ten with a better kicker, a flush, or even a full house. However, by betting, you will cause some timid players to call with a queen or an overpair, which they probably would not have bet. So it is better to bet here, even if you think you are a slight underdog if you are called, rather than to check and call as an even bigger underdog.

Finally, you should check and fold when you are a definite underdog, think a bluff would be unprofitable, and do not think the probability that your opponent is bluffing warrants a call. These situations come up all the time. An example is when you have middle pair and also have missed a flush draw on the river. Against an opponent who hardly ever bluffs and normally would not bet anything less than top pair, you should fold.

Strategic Concepts
Afterthought

Armed with the ideas we already have covered — not to mention those still to come — along with a fair amount of playing experience against reasonable competition, you should be well on your way to becoming an expert hold'em player. But keep in mind that to be successful at poker, you must maintain a great deal of discipline. This is difficult at times, especially in Texas hold'em.

Also be forewarned that the very knowledge you have acquired could be your downfall. Too often, players apply sophisticated plays at the wrong times, and it even seems as though some hold'em players try sophisticated strategies just to impress their opponents. Needless to say, this is not winning poker, no matter what the game. But the penalty can be especially high in hold'em, since your chances of drawing out on your opponents are not as great as they are in many other forms of poker. Do not allow yourself to fall into this trap.

Also remember that no matter how well you play, you will have some losing nights. (See *Gambling Theory and Other Topics* by Mason Malmuth for an explanation of why this is so.) However, if you begin to play poorly, either by losing your discipline or by trying lots of sophisticated plays when it is incorrect to do so, you will assure yourself of many losing nights. Again, make sure that this does not happen to you.

Part Three
Miscellaneous Topics

Miscellaneous Topics

Introduction

So far, we have discussed a lot of different topics. Yet in hold'em, an infinite number of unique situations and possibilities can occur. Consequently, it is now time to address some of these miscellaneous topics, plus to clarify many of the concepts and ideas that already have been covered.

As you will see, there is much more to winning in this very complex game. This can be partly attributed to the large number of alternate strategies for which a good case can be made. In addition, the fact that so many cards are shared by all the players who participate in a pot makes hold'em very different from other forms of poker.

Some of the ideas already covered have never before been correctly discussed in print. This is also true of much of the information that follows. In fact, a great deal of what you will soon read is still not well understood by a large percentage of so-called professional players. Many of these concepts are not easy to comprehend, but once you master them, you can consider yourself an expert player — provided that is, that you acquire the experience that is so necessary in achieving success in Texas hold'em.

Keep in mind that many of the following concepts interact with some of the other concepts and ideas already discussed. Sometimes an idea will seem to contradict something that was said earlier. However, one of the keys to successful hold'em play is the ability to balance ideas and to choose the strategy that most likely is best for each situation. Developing the skills that enable you to make this type of decision does not come easy. In time, however, such expertise can be achieved.

Being Beat on the River

How do you know when someone absolutely has you beat on the river and you should throw your hand away? Unfortunately, you never know for sure when you are heads-up. But suppose the flop is

and you have

There is a bet, you raise, and someone cold calls behind you. The turn card is a blank. Again there is a bet, you raise, and the same player cold calls. If the flush card comes on the end, it is now almost impossible for you to have the best hand. Though you can't say for sure that someone has a flush, if he doesn't, then he has you beat already.

Another time you can be fairly sure that a flush card will beat you is when you are in a multiway pot and there are no drawing opportunities other than two flush cards on the flop. Perhaps the flop came

If a flush card appears, you are most likely beaten. It would be different if the flop came

Now your opponents may be in there on straight draws, and it might be correct to pay off a bet if a spade hits the board.

Perhaps the easiest time to put a player on a flush draw occurs when someone raises on the flop, especially against two or three people, then checks on fourth street after everyone else checks (when a non-flush card hits), but bets on the river if the flush card comes. Folding in this spot is usually correct against typical opponents.

A somewhat related play that most people miss (even those who play for a living) is to bet into possible flush draws on fourth street when you are not sure whether you or your opponent has the better hand.

Here is an example. Suppose you flop top pair but don't have a very good kicker. Perhaps you flopped jacks and also hold a queen. Further suppose there were two suited cards on the flop, and when you bet, your opponent raised.

This raise creates a problem for you. First, recognize that you can easily be beat. Your opponent could hold top pair with a better kicker, an overpair, two pair, or a set. (The action before the flop should give an indication of what he might have.) However, your opponent also may be on a flush draw and is simply trying for a free card. In this situation, the correct play is to just call and see what the turn brings. If a flush card hits, it is now likely that you are beat, and you usually should check and fold.[3] However, if a flush card does not hit, you may very well have the best hand and you do not want to give any free cards. Consequently, you should bet into your opponent again. By the way, if you are raised again, just about always fold. It is a rare player who would semi-bluff raise twice in a row.

---

[3] Against good players, the better play may be to come right out betting when the flush card appears. By doing this, you may get a better one-pair hand to fold. Furthermore, if you still have the best hand, you avoid getting bluffed out, as you probably would be if you check. If you get raised when you make this play, you generally should fold.

Continuing the Semi-Bluff

If you semi-bluff on the flop and are called, should you continue betting on fourth street? This depends on the situation. If you bet on the flop, a lot of players will call (perhaps with as little as one overcard) and then routinely throw their hands away for the next bet. However, if you always bet again, many of your opponents will pick up this pattern and begin to raise you on fourth street. Consequently, you should give up on a lot of your semi-bluffs, if not the majority of them, once the turn comes.

Another thing to keep in mind about semi-bluffing, is to play in such a manner that anyone who tries to keep you honest will make only a small profit. Being conscious of this will keep you from betting too often in situations where you will just be giving your money away.

Changing the subject slightly, suppose you flop an open-end straight draw and two flush cards are also on board. Is it correct to bet? Some "authorities" claim that this hand should be thrown away. They argue that you can make your hand and still lose the pot. However, they fail to understand that you can bet as a semi-bluff. You often would bet a small pair with an overcard kicker (especially if your kicker is an ace) that has only five outs if you are called. But when you bet an open-end straight draw in this spot and are called, you have either six or eight outs, depending on whether one of your opponents has a flush draw. Clearly, if it is correct to bet the small pair with the big kicker, it is also correct to bet the straight draw when two suited cards are present. This means that if you are against a small number of opponents, a bet is usually the correct strategy. If both you and a lone opponent check on the turn when a blank hits, indicating that you could be against a flush draw, you may be able to steal the pot if another blank falls on the river. This is especially true if you are known to occasionally check-raise on fourth street.

Here's an example. Suppose you start with

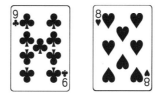

and the flop comes

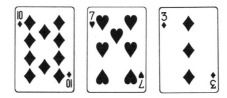

You usually should bet if no one else has yet bet and you do not have many opponents.

A hand that gives you an inside straight draw with two overcards on the flop is a strong hand. Notice that if you don't win the pot on the flop with a bet, you still may have as many as ten outs. In addition, if your overcards are high, they alone may be enough to win the pot once all the cards are out. (This can easily happen, as your opponent may be going for the bottom end of the straight.) Thus, play this hand strongly — especially against a small number of opponents — and be inclined to bet it a second time regardless of the fourth-street card.

Getting a Free Card

A related idea to that just discussed is when a bet on the flop is likely to get a free card. It so happens that against typical players, your bet will buy you this free card most of the time, providing that you are in a late position. That is, if you bet and are called, most players will tend to check to you on fourth street.

However, you must worry about being check-raised, which is more a function of the opponents that you are up against than of the cards that appeared on the flop. In fact, some players are much more likely to check-raise than they are to bet out. Consequently, as we have stressed many times before, get to know your opponents and watch how they play.

Staying With a Draw

Another idea that some so-called authorities have warned against is playing flush draws when a pair is on board. They argue that the probability of running into a full house is just too high to make this play profitable. Well, it certainly is true that you may run into a full house, but this doesn't mean that your hand can't be played. The main thing to consider is how much money is in the pot. In other words, the pot should be offering you somewhat better odds than if there were no pair showing.

It is also very important to consider which pair and off-card are on the flop. For example, if the flop is

someone already may have flopped a full house. Now you need a lot of money in the pot to continue playing a straight or flush draw. On the other hand, if the flop is

it is unlikely that you are looking at a full house. Rational players, even those who do not play well, generally throw away hands like

(In addition, if no one has bet, the best play may be to semi-bluff with your draw.)

Similarly, what about calling with a straight draw when two flush cards have flopped? Many of the same ideas apply. Basically, since you may run into a flush, you need better than normal pot odds to call. If the pot is very small, it is clearly best to fold. However, folding is not an automatic play, and the pots are large enough most of the time to make a call correct. (Also, as previously noted, your best play may be to bet.)

But suppose the board pairs on fourth street. Should your drawing hands now be thrown away? The answer is, only rarely. However, you need somewhat better pot odds than normal to continue playing. In addition, consider which card has paired and what the other two cards are. Remember that certain cards will make it more likely that someone has made a full house.

Playing When There Is No Raise Before the Flop

Suppose there has been no raise before the flop. How should you play from the flop on? In many situations, you actually should play tighter, since more possible hands may be out and you are getting smaller pot odds. For example, suppose the flop comes with a small pair. If there was an early-position raiser and a couple of callers, you could be fairly sure that no one has a third card of the appropriate rank. However, this would not necessarily be the case if there was no raise, especially if many players took the flop. A similar example is when three small cards flop, such as

that possibly could give someone a straight. It is unlikely that an opponent would play a 52 or a 75 if the pot was raised preflop, especially if the raise came from an early position.

Also consider how well your opponents play. As previously discussed, when good players have a big card they usually raise or fold, depending on their kicker. This means that if there was no raise before the flop and the high card on the flop is a jack or less, it is more likely that someone has made top pair. However, if the high card on the flop is a queen or better, a bluff may be the best play, especially if you are against a small number of opponents. (The exception is when you are against a bad player who automatically will play any ace.) Also, if one (or more) of your opponents is "weak tight" — that is, he will release a hand that the board does not hit — then a bluff is even more appropriate.

Playing When Two Suited Cards Flop

If a two flush flops, you need to adjust your play from those times when three different suits hit. Basically, you should play your good hands more aggressively, since there is a better chance that you will be called. You certainly don't want to give any free cards, especially against several opponents. Also, virtually never slow-play. If you slow-play and a third suited card comes on the turn, even if this card does not beat you, it could give an opponent a draw that, if completed, would win the pot.

If your hand is mediocre but normally worth a bet, it is usually correct to check. The reason for this is that you might run into fancy raises or be outdrawn, even if you currently have the best hand. However, you should bet on fourth street if the flush card does not come and you believe there is a good chance that your hand is still best.

Playing When a Pair Flops

Although it's a little-known fact, it is often profitable to bluff when a pair flops, especially if the flop does not include a straight or flush draw.

Sometimes, usually when you have many opponents, you can make a "delayed bluff." Instead of betting immediately when a pair flops if you are in an early position, it is often best to check. Now if a good player bets from a late position and you think he is capable of bluffing in this spot, you can call if no one else has entered the pot. Assuming that no one calls behind you, you can bet into your opponent on fourth street. What you have done is mimic a slow-play, and you often will pick up the pot. Notice that it looks as though you called in the hopes of getting some other players between you and the bettor, and you are now afraid that he won't bet if you check. Also notice that if you do get any callers between you and the bettor, your play is essentially ruined.

Here is an example of this play. In a many-handed pot, suppose the flop comes

You check from an early position, a strong player bets in a late position, you call, and there are no other players. It is now correct to go ahead and bet on the turn, no matter what card hits. Your opponent may very well throw away even a queen. (This is why you want to be against a strong player when making this bluff.) Also, keep in mind that many players would never bet on the flop if they held a six. Against such an opponent, this play becomes even better.

Playing Pairs in the Hole

Incorrectly playing pairs in the hole is a major error that causes many players to lose their money. You must keep in mind that if you do not make trips when an overcard flops — particularly if the overcard is an ace — you are in trouble. This is especially true in a multiway pot.

For example, if you have

against four opponents, a king flops, and someone bets into you, especially if you showed strength before the flop, you are almost always beaten. In addition, you have little chance of improvement. The best play in this spot is usually to throw your hand away. If no one bets and it is checked to you, go ahead and bet. With luck, everyone will fold, or perhaps someone will call with a hand like middle pair.

If your pair is JJ, TT, or smaller, it is now extremely important to bet (into a few opponents), since there are many overcards that can beat you. However, if an overcard is present on the flop and you are checked-raised, you usually should give it up. Occasionally, you might look at the turn card. (This would be one of those loose calls we talked about earlier in the text.) But unless you make a set, you generally should fold on fourth street if your opponent bets.

If an overcard is not present (thus giving you an overpair) and you are raised, you have the option to either reraise or just call (and perhaps raise on a later street). However, after you bet, if there are one or more callers between you and the raiser, then it is very important to make it three bets. By reraising, you are hoping to make the pot a two-person confrontation.

By the way, in heads-up situations, you do not automatically discard your hand when an overcard flops. Suppose you have

the flop comes

and your opponent bets. If he is equally likely to bet a ten as a king, then you should of course continue to play. In fact, you might even want to raise, especially if you think there is some chance that your opponent may be betting a draw. However, keep in mind that this is a dangerous play, and to make it, you must know your opponent well.

In addition, you sometimes can semi-bluff with a pair in the hole. Notice that you are not exactly semi-bluffing, since your hand has only a small chance of improvement. You are betting into overcards in the hope of folding out medium pairs.

For example, suppose the flop comes

and you hold

Your bet might cause an opponent with 99, TT, JJ, or QQ to fold — especially if he plays "weak tight." (Even if you don't succeed in getting anyone to fold, it is critical to bet your hand so that players holding overcards to your pair don't get a free card.) Again, if someone else bets or you are check-raised, you usually should fold unless the pot is heads up.

Remember that automatically going to the end is a big losing play when you hold pocket pairs in these situations. However, many of your poor-playing opponents automatically will make these calls, and their bad plays should prove profitable for you.

Playing Trash Hands

Suppose you have a hand like

in the big blind and get a free play against three or four opponents. The flop comes

How should this "trash" hand be played? Is it correct to bet in order to stop free cards from beating you? Or is this a check-and-fold situation?

The answer is somewhat different from what you might expect. It turns out that against typical opposition, it is a close decision between betting, checking and calling, and checking and folding. If your kicker is good — that is, if it is above a queen — a bet certainty would be correct. But if you bet, don't bet again unless you improve; if you don't improve, be prepared to throw your hand away on fourth street.

Now suppose the flop is the same as before, but you hold

110

How should this hand be played?

Since you can now beat all middle pairs, you should bet on the flop and, if you are not raised, bet again on fourth street. However, if the hand goes to the river, depending upon your opponent and exactly what the board looks like, it may be best to check. In addition, if you are raised on the turn, usually throw the hand away.

Next, suppose the flop is the same as before, but it also includes two suited cards. Now two tens should be played differently. Bet only if one of your tens is of the appropriate suit; otherwise, it is best to check. Incidentally, one reason you want to be holding a ten of the appropriate suit is that you don't want to be in the position of making trips when one of your opponents makes a flush.

Playing Against a Maniac

In hold'em, there sometimes will be a "maniac" at your table. A maniac is a person who not only plays much more than his appropriate share of hands, but also constantly raises and reraises, even though the hand he holds does not seem to warrant it. Although the maniac eventually will go broke, he does pose a set of problems for you.

Note that the best type of opponent is a loose, passive player, as he will call your bets when he shouldn't, and since he rarely bluffs, you almost always know where he stands. That is, you often can safely throw away your hand in spots where you would have to pay off other players (particularly the maniac). In addition, as pointed out earlier in the text, you can successfully play more hands against this type of opponent.

So how do you play against a loose, wild, and extremely aggressive player? First, if he acts after you do, you must be very selective of the hands you play. Also realize that drawing hands, such as

that require high implied odds go down in value, since you can expect the maniac to raise and thus limit the number of opponents that you will get. In other words, you should play hands made up of high cards and medium or big pairs, unless several people have already called in front of you.

Second, if you act after a maniac, the situation has changed somewhat. This is because when he raises, his standard raising hand is generally much weaker than the average raising hand of a typical opponent. Consequently, if you are going to play against the maniac, be prepared to reraise to punish him for his extra aggressive tendencies. A second benefit of reraising is that you increase your chances of getting the pot heads-up against him.

Playing Good Hands When It Is Three Bets Before the Flop

Suppose you have

You open for two bets, and someone else makes it three bets. How should you play this hand?

Realize that in this situation, you are almost always up against either a big pair, which you may or may not be able to beat, or two high cards, usually AK. This means that if an ace or a king appears on the flop, you generally should check and fold. However, if the flop looks favorable, be prepared to check and call all the way. (Occasionally, depending on the board and your opponent, it is all right to bet when all the cards are out.)

There are two reasons for checking and calling. First, if you check-raise and have the worst hand, you will just lose more money. However, if you have the best hand, your opponent may fold on the turn, and you won't win as much money as you could have won.

The second reason for checking and calling is that you encourage your opponent to bluff all the way. Suppose he has

He may bet this hand not only on the flop, but on the turn and river as well, hoping that you will fold. Give him a chance to throw his money away. Remember, risking free cards is not as dangerous in this spot, since you may be beaten anyway.

Now suppose the flop looks favorable, but you hold

instead of two queens. You still should play as described. An exception is when you are against two or three opponents and the reraiser is last to act. Now you may want to come out betting. This might force the players who are between you and the original reraiser to fold, since they will fear another raise.

The same is true if you hold two high cards and flop top pair. However, when you have two high cards and don't flop anything, you generally should fold, as there are just too many ways that you are beat.

Playing When the Flop
Is All the Same Suit

About 5 percent of the time, you can expect to see three cards of the same suit on the flop. This kind of flop creates its own unique problems. Let's see how some different hands should be played.

First, suppose you flop a flush. (This will happen less than 1 percent of the time.) If your flush is small, it is important to bet and/or raise, simply because you do not want to allow a free card that will beat you. Slow-playing this type of hand, as already has been pointed out, is usually a big mistake. If a fourth suited card comes on the turn or the river, depending on the number of opponents you are against, you may have to throw away your flush.

If you flop top pair against a few opponents, you generally should bet, as you cannot afford to give a free card, especially if your top pair is not large. However, against a lot of players, it is probably best to check and call. If no one yet has a flush, it is safe to assume that someone is drawing to it. You should put as little money in the pot as possible until you are fairly sure that you are not against a flush. This, of course, includes seeing that the fourth suited card does not come. Also, if the action behind you is heavy, folding may be your best option.

If you don't flop top pair but have a high suited card, you should now draw for a flush. However, "high suited card" means one of the top two of that particular suit. Don't call with something like a ten, hoping for a fourth suited card to hit the board. In addition, depending on your opponent(s) and your position, you may want to raise and try for a free card on the turn.

Against a few opponents, a suited flop sometimes will allow you to bluff. As long as your opponents are reasonable players, they won't call your bet on the flop unless they have at least top pair or one of the top two suited cards. Finally, if you are against many players, you usually cannot bluff and probably should not even bet a hand like top pair. It is better to wait, giving yourself an opportunity to see the action, as well as what card appears on the turn.

By the way, some of the same problems occur when a flop appears with three cards in succession, such as

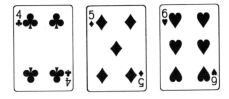

In addition, flops with medium two-card combinations, such as

also pose some of these same problems. It would be a mistake to bluff into several opponents when you see one of these flops. There are just too many ways that a JT or a T9 can hit your opponents, and it becomes almost impossible to steal in these situations.

Fourth Street Play

There are two concepts that will aid you when playing on fourth street. The first of these is that you should tend to check hands with outs and to bet hands that, if already beaten, have no outs.

For example, suppose you hold

a third suited card comes on fourth street, and neither of your aces is of the appropriate suit. Against a typical opponent, the correct play is to bet and then fold if you are raised. Notice that if your opponent does not have a flush, you are not giving him a free card that might beat you. However, if he has a flush, you probably will be raised, and you usually can safely throw away your hand.

The reason you can throw away your hand for a raise is that when you bet, the third suited card on the board will look just as scary to your opponent as it does to you. Consequently, it is unlikely for you to be raised (by a typical player) unless you are now against a completed hand. Notice that this play takes you out of a guessing game. Had you checked, you might have enticed your opponent to bluff, but it would have cost you two bets to keep him honest.

For similar reasons, you should bet an overpair when a smaller pair is on board. Again, if you are raised, you can discard your hand. An exception to this (as discussed earlier) is when your overpair is either aces or kings and you think you can induce your opponent to bluff. When you hold either of these high pairs, giving a free card is not as dangerous.

Now suppose that when the third suited card hits on fourth street, you make two pair. In this case, you have outs. That is, you can make a full house, which will beat a flush, so this situation is much different. If you bet and are raised, you can be fairly sure that you are up against a flush, and you'll wish that you hadn't bet. Consequently, the best play is usually to check and call.

Here's an example. Suppose you start with

and on fourth street, the board is

If you are first to act, you generally should check and call.

However, you should not always check two pair on the turn when a third suited card hits. Suppose your opponent checks to you, and you think it is unlikely that he would check a flush, because he would be afraid that you may not bet. In this case, you should put the chips in the pot. However, if you are against two or more opponents and are first to act, a check is probably the correct play.

A related strategy occurs when you have two pair or a set on the turn, a third suited card hits, and your opponent bets into you. The correct play usually is to raise. Unless your opponent has the nut flush, the typical player almost always will just call, even if he has a flush. (If he has the nut flush, your opponent might wait until all the cards are out and then try to check-raise.) Now, on the river, if the board pairs and gives you a full house, you should bet after your opponent checks. However, if you do not improve, check behind your opponent when he checks.

Notice that if you hold the worst hand, playing in this fashion will cause you to lose the same amount of money. However, if you improve to a full house, you often gain an extra bet. Another benefit of this play (when you hold two pair) is that your opponent may fold top pair or an overpair and thus cannot draw out on you. (Also, you should play your hand similarly if you hold two aces and one of your aces is of the appropriate suit.)

The second important concept concerning fourth-street play is that you should bet good hands on the flop and then check-raise a lot on the turn. In fact, this should be routine strategy, since you will be giving up on many hands on fourth street. That is, you won't follow through on most of your semi-bluffs and/or the other weak hands that you routinely bet on the flop. Therefore, to avoid giving your hand away, you also must check a lot of good hands. Specifically, you probably should check on fourth street as much as 60 percent of the time with your good and bad hands alike, as long as free cards are not a major problem and your opponents are aggressive.

What you are doing is balancing your strategy. Because you are such a threat to check-raise, your more observant opponents will be afraid to bet on the turn after you have checked, thus giving you a free card when you don't have much. Meanwhile, your less observant opponents will be frequently check-raised when you have checked a good hand. By playing this way, you have the best of both worlds.

Here's an example. Suppose you start with

and the flop is

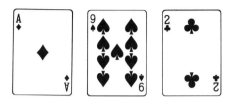

You have bet on the flop, been called, and have every reason to believe that you have the best hand. If a blank hits on fourth street, which means it is still likely that you have the best hand, you frequently should check and be prepared to check-raise if someone else bets.

Another advantage to checking a lot of good hands on fourth street is that when you don't have a good hand, depending on the board and what hits on the river, you may be able to steal on the end if both you and your opponent check on the turn. (A word of caution though. Many players are more prone to call your bet if you check on fourth street as they become suspicious and want to keep you honest.)

Another idea pertaining to fourth street is to *not* fear cinch hands in most situations. For example, suppose that you have

and flop top two pair with a small card. You bet and get two callers, one before you and one after you. A nine — which could give someone a straight — comes on fourth street, and the first person bets into you. How should you play?

First, you certainly should not fold. Many typical players, if they actually made a straight, would try for a check-raise. Moreover, this person could easily be betting a hand like jacks and nines. Consequently, your best play is usually to raise. This may cause the player behind you to fold a hand like KQ, which is to your advantage. Notice that a king would give him a better two pair and that a ten would give him a straight.

One of the most profitable plays that expert players make against mediocre opposition is to bluff on fourth street from an early position into several opponents, all of whom have checked on the flop. This play works best when the turn card is not an overcard or a third suited card. With little money in the pot, your opponents will not want to call with less than top pair, as they will fear you may have been sandbagging on the flop. Meanwhile, it is *unlikely* that an opponent will have top pair, since he would have bet it. The expert is getting 2-to-1 or 3-to-1 odds on this play, and it works about half the time. This play alone can account for a large portion of your ultimate winnings.

Miscellaneous Topics

Afterthought

One point that we have stressed over and over in this book is that hold'em is an extremely complicated game. This is easily seen by all the topics that were discussed in this section alone. In fact, it is probably fair to say that no book on hold'em can cover everything, simply because so many hands are unique to themselves.

Another thing to keep in mind is that you must avoid playing similar hands the same way all the time. Some variation is needed to throw off the better players. However, as we already have pointed out, a lot of deception is not necessary against the weaker players. Against this type of opponent, solid play is usually best. It will get the money.

Also, a lot of the fancier strategies that we have discussed are correct only when the situation and/or conditions are right. Don't fall into the trap of making a lot of great plays just to make great plays. You should be trying to win the most money, not to impress everyone at the table.

Part Four

Playing in Non-Standard Games

Playing in Non-Standard Games

Introduction

So far we have addressed what may be called "standard games." Defining this more clearly, a standard game is one of standard structure (blinds and bet sizes), which is played moderately tight and includes perhaps two or three fairly good players. Obviously, this is not always the case. Sometimes the game may be loose; sometimes it may be extremely tight. In addition, the game may become short-handed, or perhaps someone voluntarily may put up an extra large blind — known as a straddle — so that he can "gamble." Finally, the structure may be "spread limit," where bets can be any amount between (and including) two specified limits.

All of these non-standard games require strategy changes for your play to remain optimal. This doesn't mean that you should disregard everything we have covered. In fact, the material we have presented should be your foundation to winning play, no matter what game you may be in. Nevertheless there are several additional situations that still must be discussed, and in the chapters that follow, we provide some guidelines to help you when the game is what we call "non-standard."

Playing in Loose Games

Occasionally, you will find yourself in a loose, passive game. These are the very best games to be playing in, and they are usually a function of the opponents that you are up against. (At the time of this writing loose, passive games are quite prevalent in areas where hold'em recently has been legalized. One reason for this is that many players have discovered that any two cards can win. However, even though this is true, playing any two cards all the time is a sure way to go broke quickly.)

In a loose passive game, the basic mistake that your opponents most likely will make is calling when they should fold. Consequently, you rarely should bluff, especially if several players are still in the pot when all the cards are out.

There are, however, two exceptions to this. The first exception, already mentioned in the text, is when you think your opponent also might have a busted hand. Even a loose player won't call with absolutely nothing (when he has no chance to improve).

The second exception occurs when some of your opponents begin to realize that you never bluff. This means that an occasional out-of-line play is correct if it ensures that you will continue to get a good deal of action. Just remember that this type of bluff does not have to be made often. Even poor players sometimes have very long memories.

The same is true of semi-bluffing. Many of the plays we have discussed are profitable only when there is a reasonable chance that your opponent(s) will fold. If that is not the case, you also should give up on most of your semi-bluffs.

We recommend giving up on "most" of your semi-bluffs but not on all of them, because this type of bet with a fairly good hand still may be correct. After all, against weak-playing opponents, you actually may have the best hand. However, keep in mind that for this play to be correct, your hand must have quite a few outs.

One type of hand that goes up in value in loose, passive games is the drawing hand. This hand should be played and often bet, no matter what your position, especially if it has the potential to make a big hand. This is because you usually can get the heavy action that a drawing hand requires to be profitable.

Another idea that is almost always correct to implement in loose, passive games is to *not* play deceptively or disguise your hand. This means, for instance, that it is generally wrong to slow-play. However, an exception exists when you hold a monster hand and the person on your immediate right bets in a multiway pot. If many players are behind you, it is best to just call.

One play that is crucial in loose, passive games is the check-raise. In fact, you should check-raise more than in a normal game, simply because there are usually so many players in the pot. Consistent with this idea is that you almost always should be trying to thin out the competition. Specifically, when there are more cards to come, you frequently should raise a bettor on your right to knock out the other players, even if you are somewhat doubtful as to whether you have the bettor beat. (If you are first to act with a hand that "wants" to thin out the field, and you think a bet will come from your right, then your best option is to try for a check-raise.)

Surprisingly, another play that works in both loose and tough games is to raise when you flop a four flush with two overcards and the player on your immediate right bets. Your raise may enable you to win by making a high pair, which will be the probable best hand against just one opponent.

An additional concept to keep in mind is that when all the cards are out, a raise may be correct against a bettor who is prone to bluff, even if you are a small underdog to win the pot. The reason for raising is to make sure that there are no overcalls that could beat you.

Playing in
Extremely Tight Games

An extremely tight game can still be profitable, unless the game has no significant ante and/or blinds. In a normal structure, the profit comes not so much from stealing blinds before the flop, but rather from stealing on the flop and on fourth street. In a very tight game, you almost always should bet against one opponent when you flop little or nothing. When you are against more than one opponent and have nothing, the better play is to check on the flop — especially if you are in early position — and see whether your opponents bet. If they do, you should fold. If they don't, you should try to steal the pot on fourth street, except perhaps if an overcard falls.

Realize that your profits from these extremely tight games come mainly from your bluffs. You can't expect to do much better than break even on your legitimate hands, since your average starting hands will be worse than your opponents' starting hands. (You want to play as many hands as you can in a game like this to give you maximum bluffing opportunities.) One word of warning: If your opponents are tough players, as well as being extremely tight, forget about the game. The strategy given will now fail, as your opponents constantly will trap you into bluffing by checking good hands. Leave this game to the world champions.

Playing Against a Live Straddle

Occasionally when someone decides to "gamble," he will put up what is known as a "live straddle." Specifically, the player just to the left of the big blind will post an additional blind that is double the size of the big blind. For example, in a $10-$20 game, the live straddle would be $20. This play is not recommended. However, some significant strategy changes are required when one of your opponents posts a straddle.

To begin with, notice that it is now virtually impossible to steal the blinds. Consider the $10-$20 game. Suppose you bring it in for $30. It is a rare player who would post a $20 blind and then not call for just $10 more. In fact, most players who post a straddle will call for an additional $20, no matter what they hold. (Remember, they came to gamble.)

This means that you should raise only with legitimate raising hands. Semi-steal plays before the flop, which are normally so important to winning hold'em, will not work in this situation. Moreover, you don't want to make the pot so large that it becomes correct to draw to gut shots, bottom pairs, and so forth. Consequently, it is generally correct to raise less frequently with big pairs and big unsuited cards than it would be if there were no live straddle.

Also be aware that your implied odds will not be as good, since it will cost you more to play compared to what you can expect to win. As a result, you should call with fewer hands. Specifically, throw away hands like

129

and

unless you are in a late position.

Notice that we have just recommended that you play tighter against a live straddle, even though there is more money in the pot. An example will show that this is correct. Suppose you are playing in a crazy $10-$20 hold'em game, where there are not only the standard $5 and $10 blinds, but also blinds of $20, $30, and $40. Further suppose that the first person not already in the pot could call only the $40. Clearly, if you played only the "nuts" (or extremely strong hands) in this game, you would be a winner. This is because of the large overlay that you would be getting when you did enter the pot. However, if you played super tight, in a standard game, you would not be in enough pots to show a profit.

Playing in
Short-Handed Games

We no doubt could write another book on short-handed play. Moreover, correct approaches to certain situations that commonly come up when playing short-handed could be endlessly debated. Nevertheless, we will try to provide a few ideas that should be helpful.

Short-handed play is very similar to being at a full table after several people have passed. This means that much of the material already discussed about late-position play is also applicable to short-handed games.

Specifically, when playing short-handed, it is very important to be aware of your position and the position(s) of the other player(s). Of course, this is also true in a full ring game, but it is of paramount importance in a short-handed game.

For instance, when someone opens, he is much more likely to be on a steal, which means that he is less likely to have anything good after the flop. Consequently, you must call often enough on the flop to stop an opponent from stealing too much. If you fold every time you don't have a pair, a draw, or overcards, then you are not calling (or raising) enough in a heads-up pot.

How often you should call, bet, or raise, on the flop (and on the other streets) when you don't have a hand is not an easy decision and depends on many factors, including your position, the skill of your opponent, the type of board, the likelihood that your opponent will fold (either on this round or some future round), and the action that already has taken place. In addition, try to be especially aware of those players who are quick to throw their hands away (either before or on the flop) when they are in the blinds.

Other questions, such as whether you should raise with bottom pair, are not easy to answer either. However, with the knowledge gained from studying this text, plus a good deal of playing experience, you should be on the right path to profitable short-handed play.

Playing in
Spread-Limit Games

Some of the smaller limit games are structured differently from those that we have been discussing. These are known as spread-limit games. Specifically, bets are not fixed at a particular size, and you can bet any amount between certain limits. Two common spread-limit games are $1-$4, where any bet or raise can be $1, $2, $3, or $4, and $2-$10, where any bet or raise can be as small as $2, or as large as $10, or any dollar amount in between.

Most of what has been covered also applies to spread-limit games. There are, however, a couple of differences that we would like to mention. First, you often can see the flop cheaply, meaning that your implied odds are much larger than in a game with a standard structure. Consequently, many (weak) drawing hands that you normally would not play become playable in a spread-limit game, even from an early position.

On the other hand, if you hold a big pair, you want to get as much money as possible into the pot before the flop. By doing so, you will eliminate the large implied odds that the drawing hands generally can get. (One way of accomplishing this is to bet the minimum in an early position with a premium hand, such as AA or KK. Then, if someone else raises after other players have called, you should reraise the maximum.)

The second major difference in a spread-limit game is that if you limp in for the minimum before the flop and are raised, and you are not holding a hand that plays well in a short-handed pot, you should throw your hand away. In this situation, the large implied odds that you were expecting to get are now no longer available. Those players who do not release hands in this spot are the consistent losers in spread-limit games.

For example, suppose you limp in with

and a player behind you raises the maximum. Unless many players already have called the raise, you should muck your hand. Failure to do so will prove costly in the long run.

Playing in Non-Standard Games

Afterthought

As you can see, information presented in this section is built upon ideas and concepts covered earlier in the book. For instance, playing in a short-handed game is similar to playing in a full game after several people have passed.

On the other hand, there are countless variations of non-standard games that hold'em has to offer. We have touched on only a small number of them. However, as just pointed out, the general ideas presented in this text should enable you to successfully attack almost any form of Texas hold'em that you may find yourself playing.

Part Five
Other Skills

Other Skills

Introduction

There are two additional areas that play a major role in winning at hold'em (as well as at all forms of poker). They are reading hands and psychology.

Reading hands is both an art and a science. The same is true for correct applications of psychology at the poker table. In both instances, you must know your opponents. More specifically, the better you understand how your opponents think and thus how they play, the better you will be able to choose the correct strategies to use against them.

When you are not in a pot, it is still important to pay attention to what is going on. By doing so, you will begin to understand how different opponents play their hands in different situations and what tactics they are most likely to try. Also, you can get a feel for how they think. You will see what they handle easily and what confuses them, and you will get an idea of what strategies work best against them.

Keep in mind that the concepts discussed in this section cannot be mastered quickly. Like many other skills at the hold'em table, reading hands and applying psychology take a while to learn and require a great deal of experience. But once mastered, they will become significant factors in your winning play. And for those of you who make it to the very big games (against the world champions), you must become an expert in these two areas to have any chance of success.

Reading Hands

There are three techniques for reading hands in Texas hold'em. Most commonly, you analyze the meaning of an opponent's check, bet, or raise, and you look at the exposed cards and try to judge from them what his entire hand might be. You then combine the plays he has made *throughout the hand* with the exposed cards and come to a determination about his most likely hand.

In other words, you use logic to read hands. You interpret your opponents' plays on each round and note the cards that appear on the board, paying close attention to the order in which they appear. You then put these two pieces of evidence together — the plays and the cards on the board — to draw a conclusion about an opponent's most likely hand.

Sometimes you can put an opponent on a specific hand quite early. However, in general it's a mistake to do this and then stick to your initial conclusion no matter how things develop. A player who raises before the flop and then raises again when only small cards appear on the flop may have a big pair in the hole, but he also may have just overcards or a draw and is trying for a free card. Drawing a narrow, irreversible conclusion early can lead to costly mistakes later, either because you fold the best hand or because you stay when you shouldn't.

What you should do is to put an opponent on a variety of hands at the start of play, and as play progresses, eliminate some of those hands based on his later play and on the cards that appear on the board. Through this process of elimination, you should have a good idea of what that opponent has (or is drawing to) when the last card is dealt.

Suppose, for instance, that two suited cards appear on the flop and an opponent raises after there has been a bet and a couple of callers. But he then checks on the turn when a blank hits. It is now very likely that he is on a flush draw and was buying a free card. If the flush card hits on the end, you usually should fold unless you can beat a flush. If a flush card does not hit, you may want to check and call in hopes that you can induce a bluff. However, if you were also on a flush draw, you may want to bet, since a reasonable chance exists that you can pick up the pot.

At the end of a hand, it becomes especially crucial to have a good idea of what your opponent has. The more accurately you can read hands on the end, the better you can determine your chances of having your opponent beat. This, of course, helps you in deciding how to play your own hand.

In practice, most players at least try to determine whether an opponent has a bad hand, a mediocre hand, a good hand, or a great hand. Let's say your opponent bets on the end. Usually when a person bets, it represents either a bluff, a good hand, or a great hand, but not a mediocre hand. If your opponent had a mediocre hand, he probably would check. If you have only a mediocre hand, you must determine what the chances are that your opponent is bluffing and whether those chances warrant a call in relation to the pot odds.

We have seen that in hold'em, one way to read hands is to start by considering a variety of possible hands an opponent might have and then to eliminate some of these possibilities as the hand develops. A complementary way to read hands is to work backward. For instance, if the last card is a deuce and an opponent who has just been calling suddenly bets, you think back on his play in earlier rounds. Since it does not seem possible that he would have called this far with only two deuces in the hole, he is either bluffing or has something other than a set of deuces.

Here is another example. Suppose the flop comes

The first player bets, and the second player raises. A third person, who is also in an early position and is a solid but not overly aggressive player, raises again. Also suppose that several other opponents remain to act behind the reraiser and that this player just called before the flop. What is his hand?

First, notice that he is not likely to be on a draw trying for a free card, since he would not want to shut out the players behind him or the initial bettor. Second, it is easy to rule out a set. The reraiser most likely would have raised before the flop with KK or QQ but would not play 22 from so early a position. Similarly, it is unlikely that he has AKs, AK, or KQs, as he probably would have raised before the flop with these hands. In addition, he would not make it three bets with a hand like KJs, KJ, KTs or KT. (It is also doubtful that he would play KJ or KT since they are not suited.) This leaves just one possibility: KQ. If his hand is not suited, he most likely would call with it from an early position, but would still be willing to make it three bets on the flop if he flopped top two pair.

Now for a third example. Before the flop, suppose six people limp in, the pot is then raised by a strong player, and the person on the button cold calls. Everyone else calls. The flop is

Everyone checks to the button, who bets. Three people call, including the strong player (who raised before the flop). On fourth street comes the

Everyone checks and the button bets again. There are two callers, including the strong player.

Let's try to figure out the strong player's hand. First, for him to raise so many people before the flop, he must have a hand of value in a multiway pot. Second, for him to call on both the flop and the turn, the pot must be offering him correct odds.

It turns out that there is only one hand that makes sense to be played this way. It is JTs. Because of the high implied odds before the flop, it would be correct to raise with this hand. On the flop, the pot would be large enough to make it correct to call with just a gut shot, and the 9♠ on the turn would produce an open-end straight draw, which would make it correct to call again.

When you can't actually put a person on a hand but have reduced his possible holdings to a limited number, you try to use mathematics to determine the chances of his having certain hands rather than others. Then you decide what kind of hand you must have to continue playing.

Sometimes you can use a mathematical procedure based on Bayes' Theorem to determine the chances that an opponent has one hand or another. After deciding on the kinds of hands your opponent would be betting in a particular situation, you determine the probability of your opponent holding each of those hands. Then you compare the probabilities.

Here's an example. Suppose an early-position opponent calls and then reraises. You read him as the type of player who will initially call and then reraise only with AA, KK, AKs, or AK, and you know this is the only way he will play these hands from an early position. The probability that a player will be dealt AA on the first two cards is 0.45 percent. The probability of his getting KK is also 0.45 percent. So he will get AA or KK 0.9 percent of the time on average. The probability that he will be dealt AKs or AK is 1.2 percent. By comparing these two probabilities — 1.2 percent and .9 — percent, you deduce that the chances are 4-to-3 that your opponent does not hold a pair.

Knowing it is slightly more likely that your opponent holds AKs or AK rather than a big pair does not in itself tell you how you should proceed in the play of the hand. Nevertheless, the more you know about the chances of an opponent having one hand rather than another when he bets or raises, the easier it is for you to decide whether to fold, call, or raise.

Here's another example. Suppose you have

the flop comes

and your opponent bets. If you think your opponent is equally likely to bet a ten as an ace, you should at least call. If the turn card is another ace and your opponent bets again, your play is to raise if you know this opponent would still bet if he had only a ten. This is because it is now much more mathematically likely that you have the best hand, and your raise may save you from losing to a fifth-street king or queen. (If reraised, you usually should throw away your hand.)

Finally, as this last example shows, you need to complement mathematical conclusions with what you know about a player. For example, some players almost always will call in an early position with AA, KK, or AKs but usually will raise with AK. They do not think AK (unsuited) is strong enough to want to attract a lot of players. In this case, if the player calls and then reraises, he is three times more likely to have a pair than AKs.

Another factor in reading hands and deciding how to play your own hand is the number of players in the pot. Any time that someone bets and someone else calls, you are in a more precarious position then when it is just up to you to call. In general, a caller ahead of you makes it necessary for you to tighten up significantly, because you no longer have the extra equity that the bettor may be bluffing. Therefore, when your hand is barely worth a call in a heads-up situation, such as when you hold two overcards and are trying to catch a bluff, it is not worth a call when someone else has called ahead of you.

Similar thinking must be employed when you have a minimum or near-minimum raising hand and the player to your right, who has similar standards to yours, raises ahead of you. This means that his hand is probably better than yours, and the correct play is usually to fold.

Psychology

What we mean by the "psychology of poker" is getting into your opponents' heads, analyzing how they think, figuring out what they think you think, and even determining what they think you think they think. In this sense, the psychology of poker is an extension of reading opponents' hands, and it is also an extension of using deception in the way you play your own hand.

Here is an example. Suppose you have nothing and bluff at a flop that contains a pair. You are raised by a strong opponent, who knows you would bluff at this flop. Since you know that he knows you would bluff at this flop, his raise does not mean that he has a good hand. Consequently, because your opponent might also be bluffing, the correct play may be for you to reraise and then to bet again on the turn if necessary.

This brings up another point. The above play works because you are against a strong player whose thinking makes sense. A weak player is a different story. Just as you can't put a weak player on a hand, you can't put him on a thought either. When a pair flops, a weak player might raise (after you bet) with a small pair in his hand, hoping to get a free card that would allow him to draw out on his opponent, who "obviously" has trips.

Very sophisticated hold'em can go even beyond this third level. For example, suppose two suited cards flop and there is a bet from an early position. A strong player, who thinks his opponent is probably on a flush draw (since this player likes to check-raise a lot when he has a legitimate hand), may now raise with bottom pair and then bet on fourth street. His opponent may realize this and try to check-raise with a flush draw on the turn. The initial raiser now may comprehend this possibility and call his opponent down. When the hand is over, assuming that the flush card does not come, if the initial raiser is actually against a flush draw, his calls will look fantastic to some

144

opponents. Conversely, if it turns out that the first bettor really has a hand, the calls will look like a sucker play.

At the expert level of hold'em, the "skill" of trying to outwit your opponent sometimes can extend to so many levels that your judgment may begin to fail. However, in ordinary play against good players, you should think at least up to the third level. First, think about what your opponent has. Second, think about what your opponent thinks you have. And third, think about what your opponent thinks you think he has. Only when you are playing against weak players, who might not bother to think about what you have and who almost certainly don't think about what you think they have, does it not necessarily pay to go through such thought processes. Against all others, this is crucial to successful play, since deception is a big part of the game.

Several other important ideas play major roles in the psychology of poker. To begin with, when an opponent bets in a situation where he is sure that you are going to call, he is not bluffing. For example, suppose that you bet when all the cards are out and a player raises you. It is rare to find an opponent who is capable of raising on the end as a bluff. Similarly, if you raise when all the cards are out and your opponent reraises, you usually should fold, unless your hand can beat some of the legitimate hands with which he might be raising.

However, folding is not necessarily correct on fourth street. Tough players will raise on the turn if they hold a mediocre hand that has some potential to become a very strong hand. An example is middle pair on the flop that has now picked up a flush draw. Those of you who automatically fold when raised in these situations are giving up too much. This is especially true at the larger limits, where the games are usually tougher.

A corollary to the principle we are discussing is that if your opponent bets when there appears to be a good chance that you will fold, he may very well be bluffing. What this means in practice is that if your opponent bets in a situation where he thinks he might be able to get away with a bluff, you have to give more consideration to calling him, even with a mediocre hand.

An example is when no one bets on the flop and a small card hits on the turn. If one of your opponents now bets, and he is the type of player who would try to pick up the pot with nothing, it may be correct to call with a relatively weak hand.

In deciding whether to bet, it is equally important to consider what your opponent thinks you have. If your opponent suspects a strong hand, you should bluff more. However, you should not bet a fair hand for value in this situation.

An example would be when you reraise before the flop with

three rags come on the flop, and the last card is a king. If you have been betting all the way, it would be difficult for anyone to call on the end with only a small pair.

Conversely, if you know your opponent suspects that you are weak, you should not try to bluff, as you will get caught. But you should bet your fair hands for value.

Varying your play and making an "incorrect" play intentionally are also part of the psychology of hold'em, because you are trying to affect the thinking of your opponents for future hands. For example, you occasionally can make it three bets before the flop with a hand like

Assuming that your opponents see your hand in a showdown, they should be less inclined to steal against you in a similar situation when rags flop. Also, you are taking advantage of the impression you created to get paid off later when you bet with a legitimate reraising hand.

Another example of this type of play is to throw in an extra raise early in a hand with cards that don't really warrant it in order to give the *illusion of action*. For instance, you can occasionally raise the pot with a hand like

This play costs only a fraction of a bet in mathematical expectation but gains you a tremendous amount in future action on subsequent hands.

There are also other ways to affect your opponents' play on future hands in limit hold'em. For example, you may want to make what you think is a bad call if you believe this play will keep other players from running over you. If you find that you have been forced to throw away your hand on the end two or three times in a row, you must be prepared to call the next time with a hand that you normally wouldn't call with. This is because you can assume that your opponents have noticed your folding and are apt to try to bluff you.

A less obvious situation where you should think of the future is to sometimes check a good hand in early position on the flop and then check it again on fourth street, even if there was no bet on the flop. Not only may you catch someone stealing on fourth street, but this check also might allow you to steal the pot on fifth street in a future hand when there has been no betting up to that point (especially when an irrelevant card hits the board). This "slightly bad" play will not work for most players. But it can work for you if your opponents know you are capable of checking a big hand twice. Thus someone with a mediocre hand may not call on the end.

Here's an example. Suppose you are in a blind position in a multiway pot and call a raise before the flop with

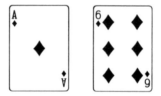

The flop comes

Since giving a free card does not appear to be dangerous, this is the type of hand that you may want to check twice if no one bets. Remember, this is a slightly bad play. But as just stated, it can work for you both in this hand *and* in future hands, where you now can steal a pot on fifth street after checking twice.

In general, you should evaluate any play you make on its merits alone, that is, on its expectation in a given situation. However, you occasionally might want to do something that is theoretically incorrect to create an impression for the future. Once you have opponents thinking one way, you can take advantage of that thinking later.

Finally, keep in mind that these types of plays will work against players who are good enough to try to take advantage of their new-found knowledge, but who are not good enough to realize that you know this and that they should therefore ignore it. In hold'em, as in all poker games, there seems to be a large group of players who like to "realize things." You must know how these people think and whether they are thinking only on the level that you are giving them credit for. If they think on a still higher level, you have to step up to that level.

Other Skills
Afterthought

As you have just seen, reading hands and psychology are extremely important aspects of Texas hold'em. Put another way, this game is too complex to play by rote. If you always play a certain hand in a certain position a certain way, your game can use a lot of improvement. You must take into account your opponents, how the current hand has been played, how former hands were played, your opponents' perceptions of you, and so on. If you don't consider these factors, you may be able to win, but you never will achieve expert status.

Many of the concepts in this section are most powerful against decent players — that is, players who play in predictable patterns and who are capable of realizing things when at the poker table, especially if they play "weak tight." Against bad players, straightforward play is usually the best approach, and against extremely good players, these ideas probably will only keep you about even with them.

Finally, some players put too much emphasis on the two topics just covered. They are certainly very important, but they are just some of the weapons that the expert has in his hold'em arsenal. Skill in reading hands and psychology, combined with all the other ideas and concepts that we have addressed, will produce a top player. But as we have stated before, this requires a great deal of thinking about the game and lots of experience playing Texas hold'em.

Part Six

Questions and Answers

Questions and Answers

Introduction

We have covered a great deal of material in this book. However, for many people, reading and learning can be two different things. Consequently, to help you retain some of the more significant ideas, we have reiterated them in a question-and-answer format.

We suggest that after you have read and studied the text, you try to answer the following questions. You probably will want to go over them many times. In addition, we suggest that you cover the answer that immediately follows each question. Only look at the solution after you have answered the question to the best of your ability.

Also, we want to point out that what follows is not a substitute for the text. In fact, some of the ideas in the text are not contained here. But enough material is included so that after you have thoroughly digested the text, the questions should help keep your seven-card stud game sharp.

Finally, the questions and answers are organized by topics covered in the text, so you can easily return to the appropriate section for a fuller explanation.

The First Two Cards:
Early Position

1) What hands normally can be played in early position?
Groups 1-4.

2) In loose games, as long as the players are not too aggressive?
Also Group 5.

3) In tough games?
Groups 1-3.

4) What do we mean when we refer to a game as loose?
A game without much before-the-flop raising and with many players in most pots.

5) What do we mean when we say tough game?
A game where there is a lot of raising but not many large multiway pots.

6) Why should you occasionally add a few hands (not in these groups) to those you play up front?
To throw your opponents off.

7) Why would you occasionally play a hand like 7♠6♠ up front?
To stop your more observant opponents from stealing against you when "rags" flop.

8) What hands do you play if there is a raise to your right?
Normally only those in Groups 1 and 2.

9) If there is a raise to your right and the game is loose?
Groups 1-3. (Beware of AQ.)

10) If there have been callers, what hands do you raise with?
   Groups 1 and 2, plus some other hands at random.

11) If no one has yet called, what hands do you raise with?
   AA, KK, QQ, AK, and AQ.

12) If no one has yet called, raise approximately two-thirds of the time with which big hands?
   AKs, AQs, AJs, and KQs.

13) Raise approximately one-third of the time with a hand like what?
   T♣9♣.

14) Assuming that you called with a larger suited connector, if there is a raise to your left, what do you reraise with?
   AKs and possibly AQs. In addition, if a lot of people are in the pot, you sometimes can reraise with a hand like J♦T♦.

15) What else can be said about the hands you can play up front in loose games?
   You should keep in mind that some hands, such as 8♠7♠ or a small pair, play well against many opponents. If there are usually a lot of callers but not much raising, these types of hands become playable in early position.

16) What if no one has opened and you have two jacks. How should this hand be played?
   Raise in a tight game but just call in a typical or loose game.

17) What if the pot has been raised and reraised and you have two jacks?
   You should now fold. This is also correct in a middle or late position.

18) What if you have opened with two jacks and the pot is raised and reraised behind you?

You can go ahead and call. Since it is now only two bets to you rather than three bets as in question No. 17, you are probably getting sufficient implied odds to flop a set.

The First Two Cards: Middle Position

1) Which hands can you play from middle position?
In an unraised pot, you can play hands in Groups 1-5 in most games and hands through Group 6 in loose games. When a player has already called in front of you, whether you play a marginal hand depends on how skilled he is. This is an important concept.

2) If the pot already has been raised, what hands should you reraise with?
AA, KK, QQ, AKs, AK, and occasionally other good hands, such as T♣9♣ or 8♦8♥.

3) What if you are first in with a large suited connector?
Almost always raise.

4) If you are first in, which hands should you raise with?
Hands in Groups 1, 2, and 3.

5) When there are callers, don't always raise with which hands?
Those in Group 3.

6) If five or six players have passed and no one has yet entered the pot, which hands should you raise with?
Hands in Groups 1-6.

The First Two Cards: Late Position

1) What hands do you raise with when you are the first one in?
   Any hand that you should play is always worth a raise.

2) If there are already callers, what hands do you raise with?
   Hands in Groups 1-3 and sometimes with Group 4 hands.

3) What if there are many callers?
   Don't raise with unsuited high cards, but be somewhat inclined to raise with Group 5 hands if they are straight flush combinations.

4) Specifically, you have A♠Q♦ and there are a lot of callers. What should you do?
   Just call.

5) But suppose that you have 8♥7♥ and several players are already in the pot?
   If no one has yet raised, then raising is all right.

6) What is another reason to raise?
   If you think it may "buy you the button."

7) Can you ever raise with some weaker hands in late position?
   Yes.

8) When would it be correct to do so?
   When you are against just one or two callers who did not enter the pot from the early positions, and you have a playable hand that you would prefer to play against a small number of opponents.

9) Give some examples of this type of hand.
   Hands like A7s, KJ, QJ, and even as weak as QT.

10) What is one of the reasons for making this type of raise?
    Against weak opposition, it allows you to take control of the pot. That is, if your opponents do not flop a hand, a bet often will enable you to steal the pot. In addition, if you chose not to bet on the flop, your raise may have gained you a free card.

11) To call a raise cold, what kind of hand is needed?
    A very good hand, even in late position.

12) If there are many cold callers, what additional hands can you cold call a raise with?
    Hands such as T♦9♦ or 8♣8♠.

13) Always reraise in this situation with which hands?
    Group 1 hands.

14) When do you reraise with Group 2, Group 3, and sometimes Group 4 hands?
    When your opponent is the first one in from a late position and he enters the pot with a raise.

15) Is it ever correct to call in this situation?
    No. You either should reraise or fold before the flop.

16) If you are dead last, what hands can you call with?
    Those in Groups 1-7.

17) What if you have a small pair and are against four or more callers?
    The correct play is to sometimes raise.

18) What does this raise do for you?
It makes the pot much larger, so that if you hit your hand, your opponents may be more inclined to call you with just overcards on the flop. In addition, they may check to you, thus giving you a free card.

19) With what other hands is this type of play sometimes correct?
Small suited connectors.

20) If you are on the button and there are many players, what additional hands can you call with?
Those in Group 8 or worse, for example, Q♦5♦.

21) Would you ever make this button call with a hand like 9♣6♦?
No, as it is too weak.

22) If no one has called, what can you raise the blind with from last position?
Hands in Groups 1-8.

23) Can you open on the button with a hand like A♦6♣?
Yes. You still should raise if the players in the blinds are either very tight or very weak.

The First Two Cards: Live Blinds

The following questions assume that you are in one
of the blind positions.

1) If no one else has raised, what hands should you raise with?
Only extremely good hands.

2) Should you raise with very good hands against one or two
aggressive opponents who have just called?
No. Your best play usually is to call.

3) Why is this your best play?
Because you possibly can try for a check-raise later.

4) Do you have to hit your hand for a check-raise to be the
correct play?
No, you just need to be fairly sure that the flop did not help
anyone.

5) If you hold AK in the big blind and are called by only one
or two players from late positions, what should you do?
Raise.

6) When is another time that it is correct to raise in the big
blind?
When several people have called and you hold a hand like
JTs, T9s, or a small pair.

7) If there is a raise to your right, which hands can you call with
in the big blind?
Only your better hands.

8) What is the problem with calling in this spot?
   Someone on your left may reraise.

9) What if the raise was to your left and a lot of players are in the pot?
   You should play more hands, especially hands that have the potential to make big hands, such as straight and flush draws.

10) When the pot is raised, what type of hands demand special attention?
   Hands like KJ and AT.

11) Why?
   Because KJ and AT can easily make second-best hands that you will have to pay off all the way.

12) If there are many players in the pot, what other hands can you call a raise with?
   Hands like 3♦3♠ and 8♠6♠.

13) Usually reraise with which hands?
   AA and KK.

14) What about when you might be facing a steal-raise and you are in the big blind?
   You can call with hands as weak as those in Group 8.

15) In the situations just described, what if someone calls in between you and your opponent, or what if your opponent plays well?
   Then you must tighten up some and perhaps play only those hands in Groups 1-6.

16) What about when you are in the little blind?
Against a possible steal-raise, you can play hands almost as weak as those you can play in the big blind. This means Groups 1-6. However, you just about always should reraise if you do play.

17) Why should you make this reraise?
To drive out the big blind.

18) What if the pot is not raised and you are in the little blind?
If it costs only half a bet to call, still be somewhat selective of the hands you play. If it costs only one-third of a bet to enter the pot, virtually every hand should be played.

19) What is the one exception?
If the big blind is a frequent raiser, you must fold a lot more hands in the little blind.

20) Can you play a hand like A6 unsuited in the little blind?
Yes, but you usually should just call.

21) If you are in the little blind and everyone else has folded, what should your strategy be?
Even though you should play a lot of hands, since you do not have position over the big blind, you usually should call rather than raise.

22) What is the exception?
When the big blind throws away too many hands.

Semi-Bluffing

1) What is a semi-bluff?
   A bet with a hand which, if called, does not figure to be the best hand at the moment but has a reasonable chance of outdrawing those hands that initially called it.

2) Give some obvious examples of semi-bluff situations?
   You have flopped an inside straight draw, or second or third pair with an overcard kicker.

3) Cite a specific example?
   You hold T♠9♠ against not too many opponents, and the flop comes 7♣6♦2♠.

4) When might you not semi-bluff in last position?
   When you may get check-raised.

5) Therefore, what is one of the determining factors about semi-bluffing when you are last?
   How frequently you think you will be check-raised.

6) What else might your semi-bluff bet do for you in last position?
   It might buy you a free card.

7) Give some examples of correct semi-bluff situations?
   A four flush or an open-end straight draw, especially with a pair, with one card to come; a small pair with an overcard kicker on the flop; and a small gut shot when the flop includes a high card.

8) What is a good rule to follow when determining whether to semi-bluff?

If your hand is worth a call or even almost worth a call if you check, then it is better to bet if there is some chance that you can win the pot right there.

9) What is the secondary advantage to semi-bluffing?

When you do make your hand, your opponent usually will misread it.

10) What is the third advantage to semi-bluffing?

It keeps your opponents guessing. If you never bluff, you are giving away too much information when you do bet.

11) When is it correct to bet two overcards?

Frequently, especially if you have back-door potential, unless you think a reasonable chance exists that if you catch your card, you still won't win.

12) When would you be less likely to bet two overcards?

When a straight-type flop hits, or a flop with two suited cards.

13) If you bet two overcards on the flop and are raised, should you call?

The answer depends on whether you think you will be able to win if one of your overcards hits and on the pot odds that you are getting.

The Free Card

1) Should you bet most of your legitimate hands?
Yes, to give your opponent a chance to drop.

2) Does this include four flushes and open-end straight draws with two cards to come?
Yes.

3) Should you bet open-end straight draws if two cards of the same suit flop?
Yes.

4) Should you bet top pair or an overpair on the flop?
Yes, if it figures to be the best hand.

5) What are the exceptions?
When there is a lot of raising before the flop, indicating that you may not have the best hand, and those times when you have decided to check-raise.

6) Should you check to the before-the-flop raiser on the flop?
No. Fight this tendency.

7) What is rarely a correct hold'em strategy?
Checking and then calling.

8) When is checking and calling correct?
This is correct when:
a) You are slow-playing.
b) You are fairly sure that your opponent has a better hand and will not fold if you bet, but the pot odds justify your calling in the hope that either you do have the best hand or you may outdraw him.
c) You are against a habitual bluffer.

9) Why might giving a free card be incorrect even when you are a big favorite and want callers?
Because the next card might be a miracle for someone, but it is not likely to make anyone a second-best hand.

10) Example?
You have flopped a small flush.

11) What is the general principle of free cards?
If you check and allow someone who would not have called your bet to outdraw you, then you have allowed a "mathematical catastrophe" to happen.

12) When is it also a catastrophe (though not as bad)?
When you give a free card to an opponent who would have called your bet, and he fails to outdraw you.

13) Name four other times when it is correct to check on the flop?
This is correct when
a) You are sure that you don't have the best hand and especially sure that you will be called if you bet.
b) You think it is likely that someone behind you will bet.
c) You have a hand that should be slow-played.
d) You have flopped top pair, either aces or kings, and you have a weak kicker.

14) What is a common situation where someone else is likely to bet?
You are in a two-person pot and were raised by a very aggressive opponent before the flop.

15) Suppose you have flopped top pair, but not aces or kings, and you have a weak kicker. You are in an early position, and the pot was not raised. How should your hand be played?

Against a small number of opponents, you should bet so you are not giving a free card. Against a large number of opponents, you should check and fold if it is bet early, but check-raise if a late-position player bets.

16) In this situation, what if your top pair (with a weak kicker) is below queens?

You must be cautious.

17) Why?

Because it is more likely for someone else to have top pair in an unraised pot when the top card is a jack or lower.

18) If you raised before the flop in late position, everyone checks to you, and your hand is weak, should you take a free card?

Yes, especially against many opponents.

19) What if the pot is short-handed?

You should bet if you think there is a reasonable chance that you can win the pot right there.

20) Suppose you have A♠K♠, the flop is 7♣6♠2♦, and everyone checks to you. What should you do?

Bet if the pot is short-handed. You don't want to give a free card to someone holding a hand like J♥T♦.

21) Why is betting or raising in late position with a hand that does not seem to justify it sometimes correct?

Because you may gain a free card on the next round.

22) What must you keep in mind if you take that free card?

Some opponents automatically will now bet on the river, no matter what they have or what the last card is.

23) Is it usually correct to raise in late position on the flop with a four flush?

Unless the game is tough, this play is generally correct. You should raise more than half the time.

24) Even if you can't get a free card, how many callers do you need to get sufficient odds on your raise?

Three.

25) What is an exception to raising?

If a pair flopped.

26) What should you do any time that you are in late position on the flop and have a hand that is worth a call?

Seriously consider raising.

27) Even if you are sure that the bettor has you beat, it may be worth a raise. Can you give an example?

Five players have put in three bets each before the flop. You are in last position with Q♠J♠ and are almost sure that no one has aces or kings, since you put in the last raise. The flop is T♠8♦3♥. If the player to your right bets after everyone else has checked, you should raise — even if you are sure that he has two tens.

28) You have A♥7♥. The flop includes an ace and one of your suit. How do you play if someone bets?

Raise and then bet on the turn with the intention of just showing down on the river if you do not improve. (If you get-check raised on fourth street, you usually should fold, unless you helped or picked up a flush draw.)

Slow-Playing

1) What criteria must be met for a slow-play to be correct?
   a) Your hand must be very strong.
   b) You probably will chase everyone out by betting, but you have a good chance of winning a large pot if you check.
   c) The free card that you are giving has good possibilities of making second-best hands.
   d) This free card has little chance of making a better hand or a profitable drawing hand for someone else.
   e) The pot must not yet be very large.

2) Give an example of a correct slow-play?
   You have JJ and the flop comes J♣6♥2♦.

3) But what if you have a lot of opponents?
   Slow-playing may not be correct if the pot has become large.

4) If the situation is not perfect, should you slow-play?
   No.

5) Example?
   The flop is Q♠J♠3♣ and you have 3♦3♥. Notice that there are many possible hands, including flush and straight draws, that your opponents can hold.

6) When is another time that you usually should not slow-play?
   When you have flopped the absolute nuts. This is because someone else may have flopped a very strong hand and will give you plenty of action.

7) What if you hold two aces and a third ace flops?
   You generally should bet, as there is usually not a second-best hand for your opponents to make.

8) What kind of hand do you need to just call a bet in order to reraise a raiser behind you?

A hand almost as strong as a regular slow-playing hand.

9) Give an example of this play?

You flop top two pair, and the player on your immediate right bets into you. Should a third player raise behind you, you can now reraise and gain extra bets from all your opponents.

Check-Raising

1) In limit hold'em, what is sometimes the best reason to check-raise?

To exclude opponents from competing for the pot.

2) When is it correct to check-raise?

When (a) you think you have the best hand, and (b) you are quite sure that someone will bet behind you if you check.

3) Is it ever correct to try for a check-raise with a drawing hand?

Sometimes.

4) Example?

This is correct when you think a player to your left will bet and two or more players will call.

5) Is this how a four flush normally should be played?

No. Normally you should bet if this may enable you to steal the pot. Otherwise, check and call.

6) What else may happen if you check a lot of good hands on the flop?

Some of your opponents may become afraid to bet after you've checked thus giving you a free card, and even if this free card does not help you, you may be able to steal the pot.

7) Can you check-raise semi-bluff?

Yes.

8) Example?

You have T♦9♦, and the flop is 8♦4♠2♣. You bet and are raised, and you (correctly) call. The next card is the J♦. You should check-raise.

9) Another example?

You have Q♠J♠, and the flop is Q♣8♦4♠. If any spade hits on fourth street, you should check-raise.

10) What is another very important reason to check-raise?

In games of today's structure, the bet on the flop is often not large enough, when compared to the size of the pot, to make it incorrect for drawing hands (and this includes hands like middle pair) to call. This means that you should-check raise frequently to cut down your opponents' odds.

11) What is a good guideline to follow?

If it is unlikely that an overcard can hurt you, it is often correct to check-raise. That is, if you flop top pair and your top pair is aces, kings, or queens (and you have an overcard kicker with your queen), check-raising is frequently the correct play.

12) What if it is a large multiway pot, you have top pair, but you are afraid of an overcard?

It still may be correct to check-raise, especially if you are in an early position. This is because the pot is now so large that if you bet, you can expect a lot of callers anyway. Consequently, in an effort to thin the field, it may be necessary to risk the dreaded free card.

Odds and Implied Odds

1) If the bettor is to your right and there are other players who might raise behind you, what must you do?

Adjust the odds considerably. That is, reduce your calling frequency, since there is a possibility of a raise behind you.

2) Example?

You hold A♣T♣, and the flop is A♠Q♠9♦. Fold if you are in second position, the player to your right bets, a number of players are behind you, and there has been no raise before the flop.

3) Another example?

In the same situation, fold K♦J♦ if the flop is J♠T♠8♥.

4) Are there exceptions to folding in this situation?

Yes. Exceptions are when the pot has become very large and/or the game is very loose.

5) How does it affect the pot odds you are getting if you call on the flop and intend to also call on fourth street?

Your pot odds are not as good as they appear to be.

6) When is it correct to call before the flop with a small pair?

When you are getting pot odds of 5-to-1 and there is little danger of a raise.

7) Why should you occasionally call when the odds don't seem to justify it?

Because you don't want to become known as a "folder." If you are regarded as a folder, other players will try to run over you.

Bluffing

1) When is the time to bluff?
When you think the size of the pot, compared to the estimated probability that your opponent will fold is large enough to make your play profitable (in terms of long-run expectation).

2) Should you ever bluff if the odds don't seem to justify it?
Yes, as this makes it more difficult for your opponents to read your hands in the future.

3) If you can beat only a bluff, when should you call?
When the pot odds, compared to the chances that your opponent is bluffing, so indicate, assuming that all the cards are out.

4) What if there are more cards to come?
You should adjust your odds if you plan to call all the way.

5) Give an example of a good fifth-street bluffing opportunity.
You have only one opponent remaining, he is capable of folding, you were trying for a straight, and a third suited card appears on board.

6) Give an example of an obvious fourth-street bluffing opportunity?
You are in a late position, and everyone has checked on both the flop and fourth street.

7) Give an example of a good bluffing opportunity on the flop.
You are in an early position in a short-handed pot, and no one showed any strength before the flop. The flop comes either ace high or king high, with no flush or straight opportunities.

8) Be specific.

Flops like K♦8♥3♠ are excellent candidates for this type of bluff.

9) What book discusses in detail the theory behind bluffing and calling bluffs?

The Theory of Poker by David Sklansky.

Inducing Bluffs

1) What are you trying to do when you induce a bluff?
Manipulate your opponent into betting a hand that he originally had no intention of betting.

2) When is it right to make what otherwise would be an irrational check in order to induce a bluff?
When you are against an aggressive player.

3) Example?
You hold either AA or KK and raise in last position. The flop comes with a medium or small pair, it is checked to you, you bet, and a tough player calls. On fourth street, the correct play is to check behind your opponent if he checks again.

4) Before inducing a bluff, what criteria must be met?
a) You need to be against a small number of opponents, preferably just one.
b) You need to be against a player who is capable of bluffing but also capable of folding if you bet.
c) Giving a free card to your opponent is not dangerous if his hand is worse than yours.

5) Another example?
You hold A♥4♥ and raise from late position, you are reraised by the player in the big blind, and the flop comes A♣K♦3♠. Your opponent bets and you call. On fourth street, a blank hits and your opponent checks. You also should check with the intention of betting or calling on the river.

Folding When the Pot is Big

1) What must you be aware of?
   There are times when your opponent can't be bluffing and must beat your hand.

2) What does this mean?
   Automatically calling because the pot is large is not correct.

3) Example?
   In a many-handed pot, you hold 7♦2♣ in the blind, get a free play, and make two small pair when the flop comes 7♥6♣2♠. You check, planning to check-raise, but no one bets. The fourth-street card is the Q♦ and again you check, planning to check-raise. But this time, one player bets and another calls, and then you check-raise. On fifth street, another queen hits. You now should check and fold.

Heads-up Versus Multiway

1) How do you play with many opponents?
   Less fancy. Slow-play less, semi-bluff less, avoid bluffing, and don't induce bluffs.

2) What about your implied odds?
   They have increased.

3) What does this mean?
   You should be much more apt to play and even raise with small pairs, suited connectors, and Ax suited.

4) What else?
   You should not raise with big unsuited cards, and perhaps you should fold hands like AT, KT, and even AJ and KJ.

5) Example?
   You hold K♦T♥ on the button, and five or six players have limped in. You should strongly consider folding.

Raising

1) Give five reasons to raise.
   a) To get more money in the pot.
   b) To drive players out.
   c) To bluff (or semi-bluff).
   d) To get a free card.
   e) To gain information.

2) If you think you have the bettor beat, is it correct to raise even if you risk driving out players behind you?
   Yes, it usually is.

3) A raise on the flop to drive players out will work only under what condition?
   This will work only against those players who have not yet had a chance to call the original bet.

4) Why is a raise often correct even if you are not sure that you have the best hand?
   If you do hold the best hand, or if your hand becomes the best hand, your raise may have stopped other opponents from drawing out on you.

5) Example?
   Suppose you raised before the flop with A♦4♦, the flop is T♦4♣2♠, and the person to your right bets. In this situation, a raise is often correct, especially if you think it will buy you a free card.

6) When can you occasionally raise as a pure bluff?
   When you are playing in very tough games.

7) Why?
Because players are capable of folding in big pots without calling one last bet.

8) Is this play normally recommended?
No, as it succeeds rarely and is expensive when it fails.

9) When is the one time that a bluff-raise can be used in a weaker game?
When you think your opponent is bluffing but also think your hand is even worse.

10) Example?
Your flush draw did not get there but the hand was played in such a fashion that you are fairly sure your opponent was also on a flush draw, and he bets into you on the river.

11) Give an example of raising as a semi-bluff.
You have A♣4♣, the flop is J♦3♣8♠, and everyone checks. If the next card is the 5♣, you should raise if someone bets.

12) Another example?
You can raise as a semi-bluff almost any time you pick up a back-door flush draw after calling on the flop with a pair. But again, make this play only against someone who is capable of folding.

13) How likely is it that someone will fold when you raise?
This is based on the answers to three questions. First, how capable is this person of folding a big hand? Second, how likely is he to be semi-bluffing? And third, how are you perceived by this particular individual?

14) When is raising to try to get a free card best done?
When you are in a late position and the bet is smaller than the bets on succeeding rounds.

15) When should raising to gain information be done?
Only in heads-up situations, and even then it is a questionable play unless there are other reasons for raising.

Heads-up on Fifth Street

1) When is it correct to bluff?
   When your hand probably cannot win by checking, and the odds you are getting from the pot compared to the chances your opponent will call indicate that a bluff will be profitable.

2) Example?
   A lot depends on whether you have been the bettor or the caller. If you have been calling all the way, a significant card that does not help you, such as a flush card on fifth street, may make a bluff correct. If you have been betting all the way, you might try a bluff on the end regardless of the last card.

3) What else must you consider?
   Whether your opponent is capable of folding a decent hand.

4) When is it correct to bet a legitimate hand on the end in last position?
   When you think you will have the best hand at least 55 percent of the time that you are called.

5) If your opponent has come out betting, when should you call?
   You should call only when your chances compare favorably with the pot odds.

6) To raise, how much of a favorite must you be?
   Usually about 2-to-1. (Except for bluff-raises).

7) What is another way to decide that a raise is correct?
   You should think you will have the best hand 55 percent of the time that your raise is called.

8) What are your four options when you are first to act in heads-up, last-bet situations?

a) To bet.

b) To check with the intention of folding.

c) To check with the intention of calling.

d) To check with the intention of raising.

9) Whether to check-raise (with the "nuts") or come right out betting depends on what three probabilities?

a) The chances that you will be called if you bet, assuming that you won't be raised.

b) The chances that your opponent will bet if you check, but will not call your raise.

c) The chances that your opponent will bet and then call your raise.

10) When is a check-raise profitable?

When the second probability added to twice the third probability exceeds the first probability.

11) What are some questions that you should ask yourself to help determine whether a check-raise is correct?

a) Is the river card likely to give someone a second-best hand that he might think is the best hand?

b) Is your opponent the type of player who would always try to pick up the pot if you check, but would not be likely to call you with a weak hand?

c) Is this an opponent who is afraid of being check-raised?

d) What has been your previous play in this game?

12) When is it better to check and call (without the nuts) rather than to bet?

When your opponent will bet with any of the hands that he will call with, plus with some hands that are worse (usually bluffs).

13) What else does a check do for you in this spot?
   It eliminates the possibility of a raise.

14) When your opponent will call your bet more often than he will bet himself if you check, what should you do?
   You should bet even if you are an underdog when he calls, as long as you were going to call his bet anyway, or when folding would be a close decision if you check and he bets.

15) Example?
   You have T♣9♦, and when all the cards are out, the board is T♥T♠Q♠4♠5♦. If you bet, some timid players will call with a queen or an overpair, which they would not have bet.

16) When should you check and fold?
   When you are a definite underdog, think a bluff would be unprofitable, and do not think the probability that your opponent is bluffing warrants a call.

17) Example?
   You have middle pair and also have missed a flush draw on the river. Against an opponent who hardly ever bluffs and would not bet anything less than top pair, you should check and fold if he bets.

Miscellaneous Topics

1) Give three examples of when someone absolutely has you beat on the river?

a) Suppose the flop is Q♥6♠2♥ and you have A♣A♠. There is a bet, you raise, and it is cold called behind you. The turn card is a blank. Again there is a bet, you raise, and the same player cold calls. If a flush card comes on the end, it is now almost impossible for you to have the best hand.

b) You are in a multiway pot, and there are no drawing opportunities other than two flush cards on the flop. If a flush card appears, you are most likely beaten.

c) Someone raises on the flop, especially against two or three people, then checks on fourth street when a non-flush card comes, but bets on the river if the flush card hits.

2) If you semi-bluff on the flop, when is it correct to also bet on fourth street?

This depends on the situation. If you bet on the flop, a lot of players will call and then throw their hands away for the next bet. However, if you always bet again, many of your opponents will pick up this pattern and begin to raise you on fourth street.

3) What does this mean?

You should give up on a lot of your semi-bluffs, if not the majority of them, once the turn comes.

4) Suppose you flop an open-end straight draw and two flush cards are also on board. Is it correct to bet?

If you are against a small number of opponents, a bet is usually the correct strategy.

5) What about a hand that gives you an inside straight draw with two overcards on the flop?

You should play this hand strongly.

6) Betting in late position on the flop, are you likely to get a free card?

Yes, most of the time. If you bet on the flop and are called, most players will tend to check to you on fourth street.

7) In this situation, should you be concerned about a check-raise?

Yes. However, this is more a function of the opponents that you are up against than of the cards that appeared on the flop.

8) Is it correct to play flush draws if a pair is on board?

Since you may run into a full house, it depends on how much money is in the pot. This means that the pot should be offering you better odds than if there were no pair showing.

9) What else should you consider?

Which pair and off-card are on the flop.

10) Example?

If the flop is J♣J♠T♣, someone may have flopped a full house. On the other hand, if the flop is 9♥9♠2♥, it is unlikely that you are looking at a full house.

11) Should you call with a straight draw if two flush cards have flopped?

This depends on many of the same factors that apply to playing a flush draw when a pair flops.

12) If the board pairs on fourth street, should drawing hands be thrown away?

Rarely. However, you need somewhat better pot odds than normal. It also depends on which card has paired and on what the other two cards are.

13) If there has been no raise before the flop, how should you play from the flop on?

Tighter, since more possible hands may be out and you are getting smaller pot odds.

14) Example?

Suppose the flop comes with a small pair. If there was an early-position raiser and a couple of callers, you could be fairly sure that no one has a third card of the appropriate rank. But if the pot has not been raised, the situation is uncertain.

15) What if two suited cards flop?

a) Play your good hands more aggressively, since there is a better chance that you will be called.

b) Virtually never slow-play.

c) If your hand is mediocre but normally worth betting, it is usually correct to check. You might run into fancy raises or be outdrawn even if you currently have the best hand.

16) Can it be profitable to bluff when a pair flops?

Yes, anytime the flop does not also include a straight or flush draw.

17) How else can you bluff at flops that contain a pair?

You can make a "delayed bluff." Instead of betting immediately when a pair flops, if you are in an early position, it is often best to check. If a good player bets and you think he is capable of bluffing in this spot, you can call if no one else has entered the pot. Assuming that no one calls behind you, you can bet into your opponent on fourth street.

18) Can you give an example?

In a many-handed pot, the flop comes Q♠6♦6♥. You check, a strong player bets in a late position, you call, and there are no other players. It is now correct to go ahead and bet, no matter what card hits on the turn.

19) What should you keep in mind when you play a pair in the hole?

If you do not make trips when an overcard flops, particularly if the overcard is an ace, you are in trouble.

20) When is this especially true?

In a multiway pot.

21) Example?

You have Q♣Q♦ against four opponents, a king flops, and someone bets into you. You are almost always beaten, particularly if you showed strength before the flop.

22) Is this true if you are heads up?

No. In this case, you should not automatically throw your hand away if an overcard flops.

23) Can you semi-bluff with a pair in the hole?

Yes. You may bet into overcards in the hope of folding out medium pairs. Notice that this is not exactly a semi-bluff.

24) Example?

Suppose the flop is A♣K♠2♦ and you hold 8♣8♦. Your bet might cause someone with 99, TT, JJ, or QQ to fold.

25) Suppose you have 9♣6♦ in the big blind and get a free play against three or four opponents. The flop comes Q♦9♥2♠. Is it correct to bet in order to stop free cards from beating you, or is this a check-and-fold situation?

Against typical opposition, it is a close decision between betting, checking and calling, and checking and folding. If your kicker is good (above a queen) it certainly would be correct to bet.

26) Suppose the flop is the same as in question No. 25, but you hold T♦T♠. How should this hand be played?

Since you can now beat all middle pairs, you should bet on the flop and, if you are not raised, bet again on fourth street.

27) Should you bet the T♦T♠ if two suited cards have flopped?

Bet if one of your tens is of the appropriate suit; otherwise, it is best to check.

28) There is a person in the game who not only plays much more than his appropriate share of hands, but also constantly raises and reraises. How should you play?

If he acts after you, you must be very selective of the hands you play. If you act after him and you are going to play, be prepared to raise or reraise.

29) What is the best type of opponent?

A loose, passive player.

30) Suppose you have Q♥Q♠, you open for two bets, and someone else makes it three bets. What should you do if an ace or a king flops?
 Usually check and fold.

31) What if the flop looks favorable?
 Be prepared to check and call all the way.

32) Suppose the flop looks favorable but you hold 9♠9♣?
 You still should play just as described.

33) Should you fold top pair if a three flush flops?
 No. You usually should bet against a few opponents.

34) What if you are against a lot of players?
 It is probably best to check and call.

35) If a three flush flops and you have a high suited card, how high does this card need to be for you to keep playing?
 "High suited card" means one of the top two of that particular suit.

36) What does a three-flush flop sometimes allow you to do?
 It sometimes allows you to bluff. Most reasonable opponents won't call unless they have at least top pair or one of the top two suited cards.

37) Should you bluff into several opponents when you see a flop with a medium two card combination, such as J♣T♦3♠?
 No, as there are just too many ways that a JT or a T9 can hit your opponents.

38) What type of hands should you bet on fourth street?
 Hands that, if already beaten, have no outs.

39) What if your hand has outs?
 Tend to check.

40) Example?

Suppose you have A♣A♠, a third suited card comes on fourth street, and neither of your aces is of the appropriate suit. Against a typical opponent, the correct play is to bet and then fold if you are raised.

41) But what if you have made two pair?

The best play is usually to check and call.

42) Example?

You start with K♦3♦, and on fourth street, the board is K♣J♥7♣3♣. If you are first to act, you usually should check and call.

43) What is the correct play if you have made two pair or a set on the turn when a third suited card hits, and your opponent bets into you?

The correct play is usually to raise.

44) What is the second important concept concerning fourth-street play?

You should bet good hands on the flop and then check-raise a lot on the turn.

45) What is the reason for this?

You will be giving up on a lot of hands on fourth street. That is, you won't follow through on most of your semi-bluffs and/or the other weak hands that you routinely bet on the flop. Therefore, to avoid giving your hand away, you also must check a lot of good hands.

46) What does this mean?

You probably should check on fourth street as much as 60 percent of the time with your good and bad hands alike, as long as free cards are not a major problem and your opponents are aggressive.

47) Should you be afraid of cinch hands in all situations?
No.

48) Suppose that you have Q♦J♠ and flop top two pair. You bet and get two callers, one before you and one after you. A nine comes on fourth street, and the first person bets. How should you play?
First, don't fold. This person could easily be betting a hand like jacks and nines. Consequently, your best play is usually to raise, even though there is a player behind you.

49) What is one of the most profitable plays that expert players make against mediocre opposition?
Bluffing on fourth street from an early position into several opponents, all of whom have checked on the flop.

Playing in Loose Games

1) What is the basic mistake that your opponents most likely will make in loose, passive games?
They will call when they should fold.

2) Should you bluff in loose, passive games?
No, almost never.

3) What are the exceptions to this?
When you think your opponent also might have a busted hand, or when some of your opponents begin to realize that you never bluff.

4) What about semi-bluffs?
You also should give up on most semi-bluffs.

5) What if your hand is fairly good?
A semi-bluff with a fairly good hand still may be correct, because you actually may have the best hand.

6) What about betting a drawing hand?
A drawing hand should be played and often bet, no matter what your position, especially if it has the potential to make a big hand.

7) What is another idea that is absolutely correct to implement in loose, passive games?
Don't play deceptively or disguise your hand.

8) What about slow-playing?
It is almost never correct.

9) When does an exception to slow-playing exist?
   You hold a monster hand and the person on your immediate right bets in a multiway pot.

10) What about check-raising?
    You should check-raise more in a loose, passive game than in a normal game.

11) What if you are somewhat doubtful as to whether you have the bettor beat?
    In loose, passive games, you always should be trying to thin out competition. When there are more cards to come, you frequently should raise a bettor on your right to knock out the other players, even if you are doubtful that you have the bettor beat.

12) What is another play that works well in both loose and tough games?
    To raise when you flop a four flush with two overcards and the player on your right bets.

13) What about when all the cards are out?
    Against a bettor who is prone to bluff, a raise may be correct, even if you are a small underdog to win. The reason you should raise is to make sure that there are no overcalls that could beat you.

Reading Hands

1) What is the most common way to read hands?
Analyze the meaning of an opponent's check, bet, or raise, and then consider the plays he has made *throughout the hand*, along with the exposed cards, to come to a determination about his hand.

2) Is it a mistake to put an opponent on a hand early and to stick with your initial conclusion regardless of his later play?
Yes.

3) Suppose that an opponent raises on the flop when two suited cards appear but then checks on the turn when a blank hits. What is a likely hand for him?
A flush draw.

4) In practice, what should you try to determine?
Whether your opponent has a bad hand, a mediocre hand, a good hand, or a great hand.

5) If an opponent bets on the end, what type of hand is he unlikely to have?
A mediocre hand.

6) What is a complementary way to read hands?
To work backward.

7) Suppose that an opponent who has just been calling suddenly bets when a deuce hits on the end. Is it likely that you are against a set of deuces?
No. It is unlikely that your opponent would call this far with only two deuces.

8) Suppose the flop is K♠Q♦2♣. The first player bets, and the second player raises. A third person, who is also in an early position and a solid but not overly aggressive player, raises again. Also suppose that several opponents remain to act behind the reraiser and this player just called before the flop. Is the reraiser trying for a free card?

No.

9) Could the reraiser have a set?

No, as he would have raised before the flop with KK or QQ, and he would not play 22 in an early position.

10) Does the reraiser have AKs, AK, or KQs?

No, since he would have raised before the flop with these hands.

11) Would he make it three bets with KJs, KJ, KTs, or KT?

No.

12) What is the reraiser's hand?

KQ.

13) When you have reduced your opponent's possible hands to a limited number, what do you use to determine what he probably holds?

Mathematics.

14) How?

By counting up the number of combinations for each of his possible hands.

15) Suppose an early-position opponent calls and then reraises, and you read him for AA, KK, AKs, or AK. What are the chances that your opponent does not hold a pair?

The chances are 4-to-3 that he does not hold a pair. This is because there are six ways to have AA or KK, four ways to have AKs, and 12 ways to have AK offsuit. Thus, AK is a 16-to-12 (or 4-to-3) favorite. Keep in mind, however, that the chances can change if the flop shows some of the relevant cards or if you hold any of these cards in your hand.

16) Suppose that you have J♠J♣ and the flop is A♥T♠3♣. Should you fold if your opponent is equally likely to bet a ten as an ace?

No.

17) Suppose that the turn card is another ace and your opponent bets. What is your play?

To raise if you know this opponent would still bet if he had only a ten.

18) What is another factor in reading hands and deciding how to play your own hand?

The number of players in the pot.

19) What does it mean if someone bets and another player calls?

It means that you should tighten up, because you no longer have the extra equity that the bettor may be bluffing.

Psychology

1) What do we mean by the "psychology of poker?"
Getting into your opponents' heads, analyzing how they think, figuring out what they think you think, and even determining what they think you think they think.

2) Suppose you bluff at a flop that contains a pair and are raised by a strong opponent, who knows you would bluff at this flop. What may be the correct play for you?
To reraise and bet on the turn.

3) Would you make this play against a weak player?
No.

4) When an opponent bets in a situation where he is sure that you are going to call, is he bluffing?
No.

5) Give an example.
If you bet when all the cards are out and a player raises you.

6) Do players generally raise as a bluff on fourth street?
No. However, tough players will raise with a mediocre hand that has some potential to become a very strong hand.

7) When might your opponent be bluffing?
When there appears to be a good chance that you will fold.

8) Give an example.
No one bets on the flop, and a small card hits on the turn. If one of your opponents now bets, and he is the type of player who would try to pick up the pot with nothing, it may be correct to call with a relatively weak hand.

9) In deciding whether to bet, what else is important to consider?
   What your opponent thinks you have.

10) If your opponent suspects a strong hand, what should you do?
   Bluff more.

11) Give an example.
   You reraise before the flop with A♦Q♦, three rags flop, the last card is a king, and you have been betting all the way. It will be difficult for anyone to call with a small pair if you bet once again.

12) What if your opponent suspects that you are weak?
   Don't try to bluff, but bet your fair hands for value.

13) Should you ever intentionally make an incorrect play?
   Yes.

14) Why?
   Because you are trying to affect the thinking of your opponents for future hands.

15) Give an example.
   You occasionally can make it three bets before the flop with a hand like 7♥6♥. Assuming that your opponents see your hand in a showdown, they should be less inclined to steal against you in a similar situation when rags flop.

16) Give another example of this type of play.
   You can throw in an extra raise early in a hand with cards that don't really warrant it.

17) What are you trying to do?
   You are trying to create the *illusion of action*.

18) Be specific.

You occasionally can raise the pot with a hand such as 5♦3♦.

19) What type of players do these kinds of plays work well against?

Players who are good enough to try to take advantage of their new-found knowledge, but who are not good enough to realize that you know this.

Questions and Answers

Afterthought

Again, these questions are not designed as a replacement for the material in the text. Their purpose is to help keep you sharp between full readings of *Hold'em Poker for Advanced Players*. We recommend that when you believe you have become a winning hold'em player that you reread the text material every other month and review the questions about once a week. Also, remember to cover the answers and to think through those questions that you have trouble with. In addition, attempt to relate the questions to recent hands that you have played, and try to determine which concepts were the correct ones to apply.

Another thing to keep in mind, as has been mentioned several times in this book, is that Texas hold'em is an extremely complicated form of poker. This means that you should be a student of hold'em for life. Some forms of poker are much more simple, and you can master them in a relatively short period of time. One reason for this is that only a small number of situations can develop, and in time, you will know exactly what the correct strategy is for virtually every hand that you play. Unfortunately, hold'em is not this way. It takes a long time to become an expert hold'em player. That is why continuous review of these questions (and the rest of the material in this book) is an absolute necessity.

Conclusion

One thing that makes Texas hold'em different from other forms of poker is that most of the money is not won or lost on the first round of play. It is true that your decisions concerning which two cards to play and exactly how to play them are very important. However, this is not enough to make you into a winning player. That is why play on the flop and after the flop received so much emphasis. On the other hand, those of you who make many significant misplays on your first two cards will be losers.

Perhaps the least known advice given in this text concerns play out of the blinds and some of the fourth-street strategies. In fact, we suspect that some readers will think that we are too aggressive in the little blind and that we do not bet enough on fourth street. Rest assured that this is not the case. Both of us know not only from a theoretical point of view, but also from much practical experience, that these approaches are absolutely correct in today's modern game against typical hold'em opponents.

In the introduction to *Hold'em Poker for Advanced Players,* we mentioned that hold'em literature seems to be flooding the market. Unfortunately, most of this material is either misguided or extremely lacking in many aspects of the game. However, with the writing of this book, those problems will now be eliminated.

We believe this book will have a major impact on those of you who read and study it, as well as on the games themselves. In general, there will begin to be more tough players around, meaning that some games will be tougher to beat. We also expect this text to be a significant contributor to the future growth of hold'em, making more games available so the expert player will have more games from which to choose. Consequently, the book should benefit those of you who make a commitment to studying the ideas that it contains.

Finally, we want to mention, as our good friend Ray Zee did in the foreword, that serious players who ignore the contents of this book will simply be left behind. We believe this is true even if you currently are having a successful run at the game. This should give you an idea of how strong the strategies and concepts in *Hold'em Poker for Advanced Players* really are.

Appendix A: Probability

With experience, most players know the approximate odds of making various hands. Only in close situations is it important to be accurate. Even here, a mistake is not tragic. However, we will note some of the more important and interesting probabilities.

A classic mistake that many players make is miscalculating their chances when there are two cards to come. For instance, if a player can catch nine cards to make his hand, he knows he is a 38-to-9 underdog on the next round, assuming 47 unseen cards. However, he incorrectly doubles his outs to 18 when figuring his odds for both rounds and thus arrive at 29-to-18 (38.3 percent), a figure 3.3 percent too high. We will not bother you with the proper technique for calculating these odds. Instead, we have provided a chart that shows the exact probability of making your hand with two cards to come, assuming 47 unseen cards.

Probability of Completing Hand

No. of Outs	Percentage	No. of Outs	Percentage
20	67.5	10	38.4
19	65.0	9	35.0[1]
18	62.4	8	31.5[2]
17	59.8	7	27.8
16	57.0	6	24.1
15	54.1[3]	5	20.3
14	51.2	4	16.5[4]
13	48.1	3	12.5
12	45.0	2	8.4
11	41.7	1	4.4

[1] Flush draw   [3] Straight flush draw
[2] Straight draw   [4] Two pair or gut-shot draw

To change a percentage to odds (to 1), subtract the specified percentage in the table from 100 and divide the result by this same percentage. For example, to change 27.8 percent to odds, subtract 27.8 from 100 giving 72.2.

$$72.2 = 100 - 27.8$$

Then divide the result by 27.8 giving 2.597 (to 1).

$$2.597 = \frac{72.2}{27.8}$$

Thus 27.8 percent is the same as 2.597-to-1.

If you hold a wired pair, you will flop three of a kind or better 11.8 percent of the time. If you hold AK, you will flop at least one ace or one king 32.4 percent of the time. If you hold two unmatched cards, you will flop a split two pair 2.02 percent of the time.

If you hold two suited cards, you will flop a flush 0.8 percent of the time, and a four flush 10.9 percent of the time. Two suited cards will make a flush about 6.5 percent of the time, but this figure assumes that you will stay in with a three flush on the flop, hoping to catch two running cards.

In a 10-handed game, the chance that someone holds an ace and another card of a specified suit is about 9 percent; however, this figure decreases if you flop a four flush and decreases further if you have two of the suit. Thus your king-high flush will be beaten by an ace-high flush less than 6 percent of the time (when there is a three flush on board).

You are two and one-thirds times as likely to be dealt an AK (or any two unmatched cards) as a pair. Consequently, a player who will raise with AA, KK, or AK is more likely to have specifically AK than the other two hands combined.

If you flop trips, you will wind up with a full house or better 33 percent of the time. If you flop two pair, a four straight, a four flush, and so on use the chart to determine the probability of making your hand.

Appendix B: Glossary

All in: When all of a player's money (or chips) on the table is put into the pot.

Back-door flush (or straight): A player is said to have made a back-door flush when both of the last two cards make his hand, even though he may have played on the flop for some other reason (such as holding a pair or a four straight).

Bad beat: When a big hand is beaten by someone who makes a long-shot draw.

Blind: The forced bet that one or more players must make before any cards are dealt to start the action on the first round of betting. Also refers to the person who makes this bet. Usually the big blind is a *live blind,* which means that the player in this position can raise if no one else has raised.

Big slick: Ace-king

Blank: A card that comes on either fourth or fifth street and is obviously not of any value to any player's hand.

Board: The five cards that are dealt face up in the center of the table.

Button: A small disk that signifies the player in last position when a house dealer is used.

Call: To put into the pot an amount of money equal to an opponent's bet or raise.

Calling cold: Calling a bet and a raise all at once, as opposed to being in for the original bet and then calling a raise.

Check: To abstain from betting, but to remain in contention for the pot because no one else has yet bet on that round.

Community cards: The cards dealt face up in the center of the table that are shared by all active players.

Drawing dead: Drawing to a hand that cannot possibly win.

Family pot: A pot in which most of the players at the table are involved.

Fifth street: The final round of betting and the fifth community card on board.

Flop: The first three community cards, which are turned face up simultaneously and start the second round of betting.

Fourth street: The fourth card on board and the third round of betting.

Freeroll: A situation where two players have the same hand but one of them has a chance to make a better hand.

Gut shot: A draw to an inside straight.

Implied odds: The amount of money you expect to win if you make your hand versus the amount of money it will cost you to continue playing on that round.

Kicker: A side card.

Limp in: To call a bet rather than to raise. (This usually applies only to the first round of betting.)

Loose game: A game with a lot of players in most pots.

Muck: To discard a hand.

Nuts: The best possible hand at any given point.

Offsuit: Cards of different suits; generally used to describe the two cards you are dealt.

On the come: Drawing to a straight or flush.

Outs: The number of cards left in the deck that should produce the best hand.

Overcard: A card higher than any card on the flop.

Overpair: A wired pair that is higher than any card on board.

Pot: The money or chips placed in the center of the table.

Pot odds: The amount of money in the pot versus the amount of money it will cost you to continue in the hand on that round.

Put him on: To guess an opponent's hand and play accordingly. To put someone on a pair of queens is to read him for a pair of queens.

Raise: To bet an additional amount after someone else has bet.

Redraw: A draw to an even better hand when you currently are holding the nuts.

River: The last round of betting on the fifth-street card.

Running pair: Fourth- and fifth-street cards of the same rank (but of a rank different from any of the other cards on board).

Rush: Several winning hands in a short period of time.

Second pair (third pair): Pairing the second (third) highest card on board.

Set: Three of a kind. (This usually means a pair in your hand and a matching card on board.)

Slow-play: To play a very strong hand as though it were a weak hand.

Suited: Two cards of the same suit.

Tell: A mannerism a player exhibits that may give away his hand.

Tight game: A game with a small number of players in most pots.

Top pair: Pairing the highest card on board.

Trips: Three of a kind.

Turn: The fourth-street card.

Wired pair: A pair in your hand.